Preserve It Naturally

A Complete Guide to Food Dehydration

Reston Publishing Company
A Prentice-Hall Company
Reston, Virginia 22090

Acknowledgments

Excalibur Products, Inc. would like to thank the following companies and universities for the use of their products and information: Anna's Antiques; Cornell University Extension Service; Corning Designs, Ltd.; Cuisinarts, Inc.; The Family Living Education and the Environmental Resources Unit of the University of Wisconsin Extension; Great American Stoneware Factory; Leifheit International; Leonard Silver Mfg.; Taylor Woodcraft; University of Arkansas Cooperative Extension Service; Washington Forge, Inc.; and Western Stoneware.

Text prepared and book designed
by Robert Scharff and Associates, Ltd.

Library of Congress Cataloging in Publication Data

Main entry under title:

Preserve it naturally.

   Includes index.
   1. Food—Drying.   2. Cookery (Dried foods)
I. Excalibur Products Inc.
TX609.P724   1983   641.4'4   83-10979
ISBN 0-8359-5606-7

© 1983 by
Excalibur Products Inc.

10 9 8 7 6 5 4 3 2 1

Printed in the United States of America

CONTENTS

INTRODUCTION TO THE WONDERFUL WORLD OF DEHYDRATION

Welcome to the wonderful world of dehydration. You are about to discover one of the oldest methods of preserving food known to civilization. Primitive people dehydrated or dried grasses, herbs, roots, berries, and meats by setting them out in the sun. They learned that dehydrated or dried supplies allowed them to exist during the long, bitter winters when food was scarce or literally nonexistent. The light weight and high nutritional value of dried food also enabled early people to travel greater distances to hunt and explore.

Nearly all people of our globe were dehydrating or drying food to some degree from the dawn of civilization. Actually, the earliest written record we know stated that the Phoenicians and other fishing people of the Mediterranean area used to dry their catches in the open air. Sun drying tea leaves was very common among the early Chinese; many other early cultures were also known to have consumed plenty of dried food. For instance, when certain ancient Egyptian tombs were excavated recently, scientists found a variety of dehydrated foods, including wheat grain. These foods were meant to sustain the spirit of the deceased during his journey in the afterlife. As an experiment, some of the centuries-old grains were later rehydrated. Miraculously, they sprouted, proving that dehydration is truly a viable long-term, natural means of food preservation.

During the ages of exploration in the 15th and 16th centuries, most sailors on long sea voyages ate varieties of dried food in order to stay alive. For example, when Columbus discovered the New World, dehydrated food played an important part in sustaining his crew and in preventing any outbreak of nutritional diseases like scurvy and beriberi. As you may imagine, much of this food was excessively salted and would not be very appetizing to modern tastes. However, to these early explorers, the dehydrated food did provide the sustenance to make long, perilous sea voyages possible.

Centuries ago in our country—long before the rise of canning and freezing—American Indians preserved their produce by drying it in the sun. Fruits like apples, pears, and peaches; vegetables like corn; and meats like elk, deer, bear, and buffalo were all dehydrated and stored for the leaner seasons. And when the pilgrims came, the Indians not only greeted them with "How," but they also showed them how to dry food.

The first pioneers likewise relied heavily on drying. Dehydrated food enabled them to endure the harsh conditions as they journeyed hundreds of miles westward across the plains. When Horace Greeley used the now famous statement: "Go west, young man, and grow up with the country." in a *New York Tribune* editorial, he should have added: "And take along a good supply of dried food." Leathery morsels of dried meat (or jerky) also acted as staples for Jedediah Strong Smith and other far-roaming "mountain men" who braved the Sierra Nevada Mountains and the unexplored Pacific coast.

By 1795, the French had developed the first *dehydrator* —a device designed to regulate the drying conditions and generally speed up the food-saving process. Although crude in comparison to today's models, the French unit successfully dried fruits and vegetables at a controlled heat temperature of approximately 130°F with a *continuous circulating airflow*—the necessary conditions for any dehydration operation. It was many years before the first true dehydrators were introduced in the United States.

Dehydrated Food in the 20th Century. Dehydrated food really became a major source of the American diet during World War I. When our country actively entered the War in 1917—sending troops and a steady stream of supplies to Europe—dried food made up a good portion of nutritional supplies that were shipped abroad. Billboards of the time shouted the slogan: "Food will win the War"—and dehydrated food did its share.

Interest in drying food dropped off somewhat after the war as the Roaring '20s, "the era of nonsense," rolled in with its flappers and speakeasies. It rekindled as the Great Depression of the 1930s crashed down upon the nation. Because people couldn't afford, or often find, the supplies needed for canning, many returned to drying to preserve what food they had.

But it wasn't until another world war that dehydrated food made its comeback. The urgent requirements of war supplies and materials set off another surge of drying during World War II. Food was rationed and every bit preserved was a step toward *victory*. With the rationing of sugar and the disappearance of canning supplies, home-makers relied heavily on drying as their main method of food preservation. The federal government even developed a self-help program which made solar dehydrator plans available to citizens so they could dry their "Victory Garden" goods. In addition, many commercial drying plants opened in this country to provide the necessary food for the free world. Dehydrated produce was a practical way to supply overseas troops; it was lightweight, easy to transport, and did not spoil. In fact, dried food continues to be used today by the armed forces as well as in the space program.

With the widespread use of modern refrigeration and freezing appliances in the post WWII era, interest in dehydrating again dwindled. With the postwar prosperity and a general blanket of security covering the country, people no longer felt the need to preserve their own food. Today, however, because of the uncertainties with which we live, dehydrating is once again becoming more and more popular as a method of preserving food.

Dried food takes up much less space than frozen or canned types. For instance, as many as 60 tomatoes can fit into a quart jar after they have been dehydrated. Another advantage of drying is that no electricity is required to keep the food, unlike freezing, and little energy is required to process the food, unlike canning.

Another advantage is the convenience of dehydrated food; you don't have to thaw it out, and you won't have any leftovers. Merely take out what you need, reclose the container, and reconstitute the dehydrated food you have removed.

Dehydrated food can easily be taken on a camping or hiking trip. The small bags of lightweight morsels can be carried on backpacking or canoe camping trips. Dehydrated munching items such as jerky, dried apples, and peaches have been popular with hunters for years, and a few nibbles of these varieties can keep you going all day. These are really tasty, nutritious foods, not just empty calories.

As you read further in this book, you'll learn many more advantages of using dehydrated food. Of course, today's desire for natural, healthful, and inexpensive methods of food preservation has put dehydration in modern kitchens. People in all walks of life can dry many of their favorites in all kinds of weather at home. However, before you and your family enter the "wonderful world of dehydration," the chances are that you have many questions about items prepared in such a manner. Therefore, before we go any further, let's try to answer some of the more common questions about dehydrating.

What is Dehydration?

The most obvious question, of course, is: Exactly what is dehydration? At one time or another, we all have experienced dehydration. For instance, after exercising and perspiring heavily, someone has probably told you to be sure to drink plenty of fluids or your body would dehydrate. When you exercise, the body becomes *hot* and begins to perspire. This heat causes the moisture to be drawn out of your body through the pores in your skin. When it reaches the skin's surface, it is evaporated by the passing air currents. This leaves your body with a liquid deficiency; therefore, it can be said to be *dehydrated*.

For dehydration to take place, as you will note, two basic conditions must be present:
1. *Heat*—enough to draw out moisture, and
2. *Air circulation*—to carry the moisture off and evaporate it. To dehydrate most effectively, the air should be able to absorb the released moisture.

Food dehydration, like body dehydration, depends on these two conditions. But, unlike body dehydration (which can be harmful), food dehydration, or food drying, is done with a specific purpose in mind: *to preserve the food from spoiling in the most natural way possible*. That is, food dehydration can be defined as a process of inactivating enzymes, or removing water (moisture) from a food to a point at which bacterial and other spoilage microorganisms are inhibited from growing. Properly dehydrated or dried food can last for months without refrigeration.

There are other ways of preserving foods. Freezing and canning, of course, are very popular. Unlike these other preservation methods, however, dehydration does not kill or cause deterioration of enzymes.

Enzymes are the chemical properties found in all living things that control the growth cycle, causing them to mature and/or ripen. When you bring a green tomato in from the garden and see it turn red in several days, you are witnessing enzymes in action. What this also shows, however, is that the action continues after the food is picked, eventually causing it to overripen and decay. Dehydration suspends the action of these enzymes, putting them into a state of inactive or suspended animation until the food is rehydrated—water is added.

Perhaps the best example of the dehydration/rehydration phenomenon is the factual, scientific discovery of live fish being hatched from eggs previously dehydrated by the sun. In Africa, during severe droughts which could sometimes last for years, all lakes, streams, and ponds would dry up, leaving the eggs to dehydrate in the sun. When the rains did finally fall again, the eggs would rehydrate and live fish would emerge. These fish eggs were actually dehydrated, preserved, and eventually rehydrated, proving the validity of this life-saving process.

What Type of Food Can Be Dehydrated?

Most food can be dehydrated. Fruits and vegetables are among the easiest and most popular for the beginner. But only top quality food should be dried. Select fresh, firm, and perfectly clean food, free of bruises or blemishes. Fruits and vegetables at their peak of ripeness will have the richest flavor and be more nutritious. Immature food will lack color, overmature fruits will be soft and mushy, and overmature vegetables will be tough and woody. Many people believe that inferior produce can be used for dehydration because it will be all wrinkled up when it is dried anyway. This is *not* always true. Vegetables and fruits (in fact, all produce) should be in prime condition. The quality of the food that you place in the dehydrator determines the quality of the dried food that is processed.

In addition to fruits and vegetables, meats, fish, herbs, cheeses (including tofu), yogurt, and even pickles can be dried at home. In fact, almost anything that has water in it can have the water gently removed.

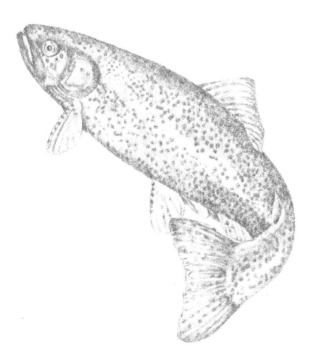

What is the Nutritional Value of Dehydrated Food?

Fresh produce, which can be dehydrated immediately, is our best source of natural vitamins, sugars, and minerals. Once it is harvested, some of this nutritional value is lost. If fresh food is left to sit on a counter in a store or at home, the vitamin content deteriorates even further. By drying food rather than holding it fresh, most losses can be checked.

With dehydrating, you preserve *more* nutrients than with methods of preservation that involve cooking food. The higher the temperature is during processing, the more nutrients are lost. Although dehydration depends on heat, it requires it at much lower temperatures than cooking does—usually not over 145°F. The effect of water removal on nutritional changes of dehydrated food is minimal except that some vitamin A and vitamin C are lost during dehydration. (This can be kept to a minimum with proper pretreatment.) Dehydrated food must also be properly handled, prepared, dried, packaged, and stored under appropriate conditions and used within one year. For example, if improperly packaged, dehydrated vegetables can lose up to 50% of the vitamin A during the first six months of storage.

What Does Dehydrated Food Taste Like?

The taste of some dehydrated food is intensified because we are removing water—not sugars, flavors, or nutrients. Herbs become more flavorful. Some vegetables, such as carrots, taste more concentrated, and any food that contains sugar tastes sweeter. Even though food with sugar tastes sweeter, the caloric value is the same as in the fresh food because you are adding nothing. Children love dried fruits such as bananas, apples, and pineapples. Many dried foods, especially those used in cooking, are indistinguishable from fresh. For example, cooked, dehydrated spinach tastes just like garden fresh spinach. Part of the variety and versatility that dehydration offers, however, is that some other foods taste different in the fresh and dehydrated states. For instance, let's consider grapes and raisins. Both these snack fruits are delicious and inviting, but each is unique in flavor, texture, and appearance. Many people don't realize that they both are one and the same; except for the fact that the grapes are fresh and raisins are dried, or dehydrated. Another example is pineapple. There is nothing better than a succulent, fresh piece of pineapple that enlivens each taste bud with every bite. But, there is also nothing like a tantalizing piece of dried pineapple with its burst of new flavor and texture which only dehydration can give. Of course, you may not care for the taste or flavor of every dried food. Experiment—you won't know what you'll like or dislike until you try it. Remember, if you don't like the taste or consistency of a particular food, it can generally be reduced to a powder and used as a seasoning.

How is Dried Food Rehydrated?

Rehydration is the process of restoring liquid to dried food. Of course, properly dried food can easily be rehydrated. It returns practically to its original size, form, and appearance. If properly handled, it will retain much of its aroma and flavor as well as the minerals and appreciable amounts of vitamins.

Meats and herbs do not need to be rehydrated before cooking. For other foods, first rehydrate and then cook as you do fresh food. While most vegetables are prepared by cooking, some such as carrots can be eaten raw after rehydration. Vegetable snacks and chips are, of course, eaten in the dried state.

There are many ways to rehydrate fruits: in water or in fruit juice, for example. Try rehydrating blueberries in grape juice or apples in apple juice. The same principle applies to fruit leathers. Rehydrate vegetables in vegetable juice like a multi-vegetable mixture juice. Some vegetables are excellent when rehydrated in milk.

Rehydrated carrots are just as attractive and tasty as their fresh counterparts.

Food Preservation Economic Comparison		
Freezing =	16.2¢/pound	
	Equipment: Freezer @ $270 amortized over 20 years*	$13.50/year
	Repairs: 2% of purchase price	5.40/year
	Packaging:	25.00
	Electricity: To operate freezer @ 5¢/kilowatt hour	35.28
	To blanch 250 pounds of food (4 minutes/pound)	1.99
		$81.17
	(Based on 500 pounds of food)	
Canning =	5.5¢/pound	
	Equipment: Pressure canner @ $65 amortized over 20 years*	$ 3.25
	Water bath canner @ $10 amortized over 20 years	.50
	Repairs: 2% of purchase price	1.30
	Packaging: 24 dozen (288) quart jars @ $4.39/dozen amortized over 10 years	10.53
	24 dozen lids replaced each year @ 49¢/dozen	11.76
	Electricity: To pressure can 140 quarts @ 5¢/kilowatt hour	1.44
	To water bath can 140 quarts	2.22
		$31.00
	(Based on 560 pounds of food in 280 quarts)	
Dehydrating =	4.8¢/pound	
	Equipment: Electric dehydrator @ $190 amortized over 20 years*	$ 9.50
	Repairs: 2% of purchase price	3.80
	Packaging: 500 one-pound plastic bags	2.50
	Electricity: For drying food	6.50
	For blanching 250 pounds of food (4 minutes/pound)	1.99
		$24.29
	(Based on 500 pounds of food)	

*If the equipment is used for less than the full amortization period, the cost per pound of food increases significantly. Also if smaller amounts of food are processed, the average cost per pound will increase.

Herbs, vegetables, meats, and fruits can be added to your favorite recipes. When doing this, keep in mind that as a general rule you should allow 30 minutes to 1 hour to rehydrate when added to a soup or a stew. Green beans are an exception; they rehydrate best when soaked overnight in the refrigerator. Small pieces of dried food need only 15 to 30 minutes of soaking. Rehydration time can be speeded up by pouring boiling water over any kind of dried food or by using one of the many steamers currently on the market.

What About Cooking Dehydrated Food?

The amount of water used for cooking should be as near as possible to the amount which the food will take up. It is better to add water during any cooking process than to start out with more than needed. Like fresh food, dried food, if overcooked, will lose both texture and flavor. Dehydrated, blanched vegetables can be prepared for the table in a short time. Fruits can be simmered to make them softer or plumper.

How Does Dehydration Compare with Other Methods of Preservation?

As a consumer, you must decide what method of food preservation is the most economical to use. The chart on the preceding page is a simplified economic comparison of the three common methods—freezing, canning, and dehydration—of preserving food at home. It was prepared—in part—by the Family Living Education and the Environment Resources Unit of the University of Wisconsin-Extension and reprinted with the university's permission.

From the chart, you can see that it makes sense to dehydrate. The equipment costs for canning, and particularly freezing, are significantly higher than they are for dehydrating. Dehydration is also economically viable because it allows you to purchase large quantities of food in peak seasons when prices are cheapest and to preserve the bulk of your garden harvest. Although large quantities of food may be frozen or canned, there may be considerable difficulty in finding sufficient space to store them. Thus as you have seen, dehydration offers a whole new and wonderful world of variety and interest in food preparation.

2

HOW FOOD IS DEHYDRATED

There are over a half-dozen different ways to dehydrate food. Some of the traditional drying methods produce excellent results; others do not. While the electric dehydrator has replaced most of the older methods, many recipe books still refer to them. Let's take a look at the drying methods of the past—most of which were contrived in the days when "pinches" were used instead of teaspoons and food was cooked until "it looked done" rather than actually being timed—to see why they have been replaced by the "magic" of the electric dehydrator.

Sun Drying. This is the original dehydration method. Commercial food processors continue to use it, but trying it at home is more trouble than it's worth. Sun drying demands near-perfect low humidity conditions and temperatures in the high 80s to assure a reasonable amount of success. And even if you manage to meet these rather difficult requirements, food dried in the sun will take several days as compared to several hours required in a dehydrator. Because sun drying takes so long, the food produced is of lower quality and nutritional value and it is at the mercy of insects, dirt, and the elements. It is the least expensive way to dehydrate food and it can accommodate large quantities at one time.

Solar Drying. Promoted during World War II, solar drying is somewhat more efficient than traditional sun drying because of the increased temperatures. It also refines the drying process by (a) a tracking system to follow the sun, (b) a venting system to control the temperature, (c) enough space for construction and efficient operation, and (d) a back-up system to provide an alternative heat source and a fan to circulate air. However, despite these apparent improvements, it is still unpredictable, slow, time-consuming, and offers no assurance of food quality.

Air and Shade Drying. Spoilage is a significant problem with both these methods of food preservation. Because of the lack of the sun's heat, drying times are extended greatly. As a result, the time required to dry the food product is generally "up in the air." That is, with this method, food is simply hung up or left to sit until it is dry for a period of time that can range from several days to weeks.

If you ever have time to spare, you might want to experiment with one unique form of air drying called "string drying." Slices of produce are strung on long pieces of string and hung from nails or rafters in a warm room. One of the most popular foods dried this way was whole string beans, or "leather britches."

Oven Drying. Although many people use standard, convection, and microwave ovens for drying food, oven drying, on the whole, is very "iffy." While generally a vast improvement over some of the older methods of dehydrating, scorching is usually a major problem. Also, food frequently comes out more brittle, darker in texture, and less tasty than before it was oven dried. In addition, normal oven usage may be interrupted for long periods of time and the energy cost is usually substantially greater than with a family size food dehydrator. Remember that standard, convection, and microwave ovens were manufactured for purposes other than dehydrating; therefore, oven drying is not usually too successful.

ELECTRIC DEHYDRATORS— THE ONLY WAY TO DRY

There is no question about it—the electric dehydrator is the best way to dehydrate food today. Gone are the hours of turning and tending, the frustration of unpredictable results, and the headaches of having to rescue produce from the rain. You can dry 24 hours a day, come rain or come shine, working comfortably and conveniently in your own kitchen. There's little rearranging to do; your dehydrator fits neatly on the kitchen counter. But while it's compact, the roomy trays hold pounds of food. This means you can dehydrate more food per load, reducing

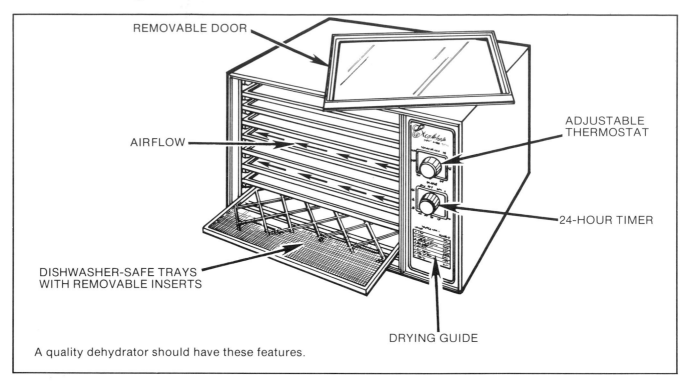

REMOVABLE DOOR

AIRFLOW

ADJUSTABLE THERMOSTAT

24-HOUR TIMER

DISHWASHER-SAFE TRAYS WITH REMOVABLE INSERTS

DRYING GUIDE

A quality dehydrator should have these features.

costs and saving energy. Plus the food is kept clean and is protected from the dust, insects, and pollutants that frequently settled on food dehydrated by the traditional methods.

The two most important features of any dehydrator are the heat source and the fan or blower. Without the correct mix of heat and circulating air, it is impossible to produce properly dehydrated products.

Heat. The heat source must be efficient and durable, such as Nichrome or heating wire coils; coils should barely glow when in use. An efficient source keeps the heat flow constant. This minimizes the dehydrating time, resulting in a better product and preventing spoilage. In general, the source should be enclosed to reduce shock and fire hazard and should be preferably located at the back or side of the unit. Bottom element units tend to be extremely inefficient; the temperature from the lowest to the uppermost drying tray may fluctuate as much as 60° to 80°F.

The wattage of the heat source must be adequate for the drying area, or capacity, of the unit. As a general rule of thumb, 70 watts per tray can be considered sufficient. Insufficient wattage can lead to spoilage during dehydration, but it must not be too great for your household electric circuit.

Temperature Control. Some form of temperature control is needed to regulate the heat source; avoid units without one. Such a control promotes consistent, even results. The control may be one of the newer electronic heat controls or a conventional thermostat.

The best controls are completely adjustable. Controls geared to just "low-medium-high" heats are inadequate.

As in regular cooking, different foods require distinctly different processing temperatures. For instance, meats require a fairly constant temperature of 145°F, whereas most herbs must be kept at 95°F or they will scorch. A variable temperature range from 85° to 145°F is adequate for dehydrating; lower or higher temperatures will either spoil or cook food.

Look for a control that is both easy to read and adjust. It should be readily visible without having to move the machine. In the event that the control or thermostat fails, the unit should also be equipped to shut off the heat source. Be sure the unit is listed with UL (Underwriters' Laboratories) and meets all their specifications.

Fan or Blower. Proper airflow and circulation are necessary to properly seal the food's surface, reducing nutrition, flavor, and color losses. When heated air is blown across the food, evaporation takes place and the moisture from the food is absorbed by the dry air. When the air becomes saturated with the moisture, the drying process stops until the moist air is replaced by dry air.

Make sure the blower or fan supplies an even heat flow to every tray. This can best be achieved with a horizontal airflow, one that flows in one side, across the food, and out the other side. Horizontal flow reduces flavor mixing and permits even dehydrating without tray rotation.

Make sure that the size of the blower or fan is suitable for the internal capacity of the dehydrator; otherwise, the food will "cook" rather than dehydrate. The blower or fan should also be designed for continuous and quiet operation. Keep in mind that you'll have to live with its sound for hours on end.

Other Features to Look for When Buying an Electric Food Dehydrator

Construction. Your dehydrator should be constructed of a nonflammable, durable material. Many wood units draw in odors and retain harmful bacteria; they also have a tendency to warp when constantly exposed to high humidity. Plastic or metal units hold up better under heavy use. In addition, plastic and metal walls are easier to clean both inside and outside. Wiping with a damp cloth is generally sufficient for cleaning most spills.

Trays, Inserts, and Doors. It is best to have trays and inserts made of stainless steel, fiberglass coated with Teflon®, nylon, plastic, or some other food-grade material. Because they could contaminate the food, aluminum, copper, or galvanized metal trays should not be used.

Meshed insert trays are the preferred type for dehydrator use because they allow air to circulate all around the food and prevent moisture from being trapped on the underside of the pieces. The screen or mesh should be well supported to prevent sagging and sufficiently fine so that food pieces won't fall through or become lodged in the mesh. Check to make sure that the trays can be covered with Teflex, kitchen parchment paper, or plastic wrap for the drying of leathers and other purees. (See Chapter 3 for more information on Teflex.)

Make sure that the trays are convenient to load and unload and are easy to clean. They should be lightweight, yet sturdy enough to hold the food without bending. Choose a unit with trays that are either dishwasher safe (when placed away from the washer's heating element) or which can be soaked. Soaking rehydrates stuck food, simplifying its removal without scraping that could damage the trays.

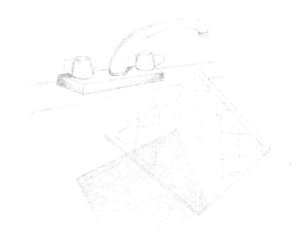

To facilitate loading and unloading, the door should be easy to open and close. Fold down, removable doors are the simplest with which to work. Most either set in hinges or rest on a guide. Swing-open doors tend to encroach on already cramped countertops.

Tinted, view-thru doors are desirable if the progress of the food must be checked. The view-thru feature keeps the dehydrating process from being interrupted, while the tinting prevents light from fading the color and nutrients of the food. Treat doors carefully to prevent scratching; clean with a damp sponge or soft cloth only.

Unit Size and Accessibility. When selecting your dehydrator, keep in mind that a large internal capacity needn't be reflected in external size. The unit should be small enough to fit comfortably and attractively on your kitchen counter, yet be capable of dehydrating enough food for your family's needs without an excessive number of loads. Average units are the size of a microwave oven; over-sized dehydrators that must be kept in the cellar or garage are simply not convenient to use. The overall weight is as important as the size. Keep in mind that the unit will have to be moved now and again for routine cleaning purposes.

Operation. Be sure to look for a dehydrator that is easy to operate. This is a major concern; the more complicated the procedures, the less motivated you'll be to use the unit. Most of the instructions for setup and food preparation should be relatively uncomplicated and should not require a great deal of expertise.

The electric dehydrator should be located on a smooth, dry, level surface such as a countertop. **Caution:** Do not operate the dehydrator near water or outdoors. The power cord plugs into any standard 120 volt/10 ampere outlet; a heavy-duty line is not needed. The cord should not be allowed to hang over the counter or touch hot surfaces. Check the cord carefully; do not operate the unit if there is evidence of wear or exposed wires.

Electric dehydrators are available in various sizes. Choose one that fits your drying needs.

Check how the actual dehydration is done. In general, the food is prepared, loaded on the trays in a single layer, and placed in the unit. The trays are not treated with any sort of non-stick product, unless specifically recommended by the manufacturer. After checking that the unit is plugged in, the thermostat or control is set to the desired temperature for the particular food being dehydrated.

A timer is a boon for monitoring the dehydrating process, particularly since recipe dehydration times are only *approximations* and vary considerably from one area to another. Timers generally run up to 24 hours and are usually considered far simpler to use than a probe control. A probe will shut off the dehydrator when the individual item being probed is dried; the remainder, however, could possibly be too moist or insufficiently dry. As mentioned earlier, the timer control may or may not double as the "on-off" switch.

The dehydration times for different foods vary tremendously. The one general guideline is to leave the food in until you can't see or feel any evidence of moisture. *No dehydrator can judge this for you.* When you're satisfied that the food is dry, allow it to cool in the unit for 30 minutes to 1 hour. (Recommended drying times can be found in individual chapters.) It is then removed from the trays and packaged in the proper storage containers.

1. Operating a dehydrator is extremely simple. With the unit already plugged in, carefully slide the food-laden trays into position. Use both hands to prevent tipping.

2. Once all the trays are in place, set the controls for the correct temperature and dehydrating time.

Economy. Determine how much food can be dehydrated in one load. The money you save by dehydrating is partially related to the capacity, or drying area, of the unit; large loads maximize savings. The more food you can dehydrate per load, the fewer loads you will need and the more time and energy will be saved. With only 8 square feet of drying area, you can dehydrate nearly 25 pounds of vegetables per day; 16 square feet of area can hold up to a bushel of apples per day.

Consider what the initial cost of the unit is and how much electricity it requires. An average 600-watt dehydrator costs about 3 cents per hour to operate. Most good units will pay for themselves within one season. In some units, rotating the trays 180° halfway through the cycle cuts energy consumption by reducing the overall dehydrating time.

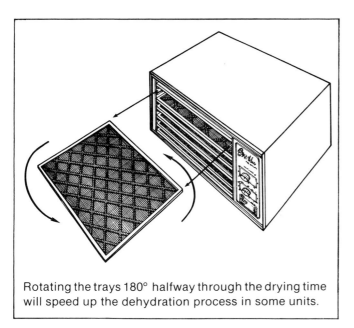

Rotating the trays 180° halfway through the drying time will speed up the dehydration process in some units.

Safety. Make sure the unit's electrical components are properly wired in accordance with UL requirements. It should be shockproof, nonflammable, and free of sharp corners, and its finish should be nontoxic. A quality unit must have all these features to be safe for home use and should come complete with some type of operating instructions or manual.

Repairability. Since even the best appliances occasionally malfunction, be sure your dehydrator comes with a warranty. The warranty should specify what parts are covered, where the unit can be taken or sent for repairs, and who is responsible for shipping costs. A reputable company will stand behind its products.

An electric dehydrator is capable of producing any of the above dried foods.

3

PREPARING, STORING, AND USING DEHYDRATED FOOD

No matter what food you are drying, given steps are involved. That's what makes dehydrators so easy to use. You only have to learn one basic set of procedures, then vary or adapt them to fit each food group. In other words, no matter what food you wish to dehydrate, the following procedures will come into play in one form or another: preparation, pretreatment, drying, testing, packaging, and storage.

PREPARATION

Drying is simple, but that doesn't mean that food can go directly from the store or garden into the dehydrator. Some preparation—washing, peeling, slicing, and/or sorting—is still required. In fact, the final quality of the food you dry will vary significantly according to the amount of preparation given. Sloppy washing leads to insect infestation, and unequal slicing prevents uniform drying. Keep an old scout motto in mind and you'll remember that the food should "always be prepared."

Preparing the Food

Dehydration is a very simple process, and as such it requires very little specialized equipment other than your dehydrator. In fact, you will probably find most of the other utensils needed right in your kitchen. Here's the additional equipment you should have on hand:

• A sharp paring knife to reduce tearing of and damage to food. This is the one absolutely indispensable item in the list as most foods require some form of cutting or slicing. Carbon-bladed knives may turn some fruits and vegetables black, so use one with a stainless steel blade instead.

• A vegetable slicer. Although you can do all your cutting with a knife, a slicer will speed up and simplify routine cutting tasks as well as guarantee that the slices will be equal. Some models come with a fluted attachment to make decorative food for dipping and garnishes.
   • A grater.
   • A bagging and sealing machine.
   • A strainer.
   • A fluted vegetable cutter.
   • Masking tape, for labeling storage containers.
   • A slotted spoon.
   • A cutting board.
• A steamer or kettle/colander combination if you will be blanching (pretreating) vegetables. The colander or basket section is also handy for washing small foods like berries.
• A blender or food processor for pureeing fruits and vegetables for leathers, chopping flakes, and making baby food.
• Teflex™, kitchen parchment paper, or plastic wrap should be used for drying leathers, granola, grains, purees, and liquid items. Teflex is a Teflon®-coated fiberglass sheet specifically sized to fit many dehydrator trays.* It can also be cut to fit surfaces such as frying pans, microwave ovens, and other oven utensils. Food will not stick to the Teflex, so it's ideal for leathers and other sticky substances.
• A corer and pitter. These make fast work of apples, pears, and cherries, but a knife can serve the same purpose.
   • Measuring utensils and kitchen scale.
   • Silica gel to absorb excess moisture when storing produce.
   • Storage containers.
Starter kits are available that contain most of the items you'll need to begin your adventure into the wonderful world of dehydration.

---

*Teflex™ is a trademark of Excalibur Products, Inc., Division of OEI.
Teflon® is a registered trademark of DuPont Company.

Year-Round Food Buying Guide			
January	**February**	**March**	**April**
Avocados	Avocados	Artichokes	Asparagus
Bananas	Bananas	Asparagus	Bananas
Cabbage	Broccoli	Avocados	Cabbage
Cauliflower	Cabbage	Bananas	Chicory
Mushrooms	Cauliflower	Broccoli	Escarole
Pears	Kumquats	Grapefruit	Onions
Potatoes	Mangoes	Kumquats	Pineapple
Turnips	Mushrooms	Lettuce	Radishes
Winter Squash	Pears	Mushrooms	Rhubarb
	Tangerines	Radishes	Spinach
	Winter Squash	Spinach	Strawberries
May	**June**	**July**	**August**
Asparagus	Avocados	Apricots	Apples
Bananas	Apricots	Bananas	Bananas
Celery	Bananas	Blueberries	Beets
Papaya	Cantaloupe	Cabbage	Berries (seedless)
Peas	Cherries	Cantaloupe	Cabbage
Pineapple	Corn	Cherries	Carrots
Potatoes	Cucumber	Corn	Corn
Strawberries	Figs	Cucumbers	Cucumbers
Tomatoes	Green Beans	Dill	Dill
Watercress	Limes	Eggplant	Eggplant
	Mangoes	Figs	Figs
	Nectarines	Gravenstein Apples	Melons
	Onions	Green Beans	Nectarines
	Peaches	Nectarines	Peaches
	Peas	Okra	Pears
	Peppers	Peaches	Peppers
	Pineapple	Peppers	Plums
	Plums	Prunes	Potatoes
	Summer Squash	Watermelon	Summer Squash
			Tomatoes
September	**October**	**November**	**December**
Apples	Apples	Apples	Apples
Bananas	Bananas	Bananas	Avocados
Broccoli	Broccoli	Broccoli	Bananas
Carrots	Grapes	Cabbage	Grapefruit
Cauliflower	Peppers	Cauliflower	Lemons
Corn	Persimmons	Cranberries	Limes
Cucumbers	Pumpkin	Dates	Mushrooms
Dill	Yams	Eggplant	Oranges
Figs		Mushrooms	Pears
Grapes		Pumpkin	Pineapple
Greens		Sweet Potatoes	Tangerines
Melons			
Okra			
Onions			
Pears			
Peppers			
Potatoes			
Summer Squash			
Tomatoes			
Yams			

Plan Ahead. How thick should the slices be? Should you peel or not peel the food? What quantity of food is needed? These questions should all be answered during the preparation stage. By deciding how you will use the food before you dehydrate, you'll avoid having to alter the food when the time comes to use it in a recipe.

Planning ahead can also help you decide what to dry. If your family is always on the run, you might want to concentrate on "portable" foods like fruits, leathers, granola, nuts, and trail mixes. These make nice additions to lunches and can be easily snatched up in passing. On the other hand, if you enjoy and have the time to cook, make sure you stock up on vegetables and herbs that will be out of season during the winter months. A buying guide to the year-round purchase of fruits and vegetables is given on the previous page.

Amount of Food Needed for Dehydrating. It is difficult to suggest amounts of food to purchase because of the variables involved. How ripe the food is, the size of slices, the amount of discard in preparation, the moisture content, and how fast the food dries all have to be taken into consideration before the quantity can be decided upon. For example, tomatoes have very little waste with a very high moisture content while apples have quite a bit of waste (peels, core, and stems) with a lower moisture content. Another thing to remember is some fresh products have a long shelf life while others have a very short shelf life. You can take up to a few weeks to dehydrate a quantity of fresh apples without noticeable loss of quality, but tomatoes will have to be processed within a few days. Depending on the model size, your dehydrator will hold approximately 15 to 30 pounds of prepared food per dryer load. The amount to purchase will also depend on the drying time and how many dryer loads can be processed before spoilage begins.

The aim of dehydration is to reduce the food's moisture content to between 5 and 20%—a range in which decay-causing bacteria can't survive. This reduction in water causes dehydrated food to be only one-fourth to one-twelfth the weight and bulk of the original food. To give a better idea as to the amount of food to purchase or pick from your garden, the chart below, prepared by the University of Arkansas Cooperative Extension Service, will give you some idea as to the amount of reduction in food produce caused by dehydration.

Selection of Produce. Many people believe that inferior produce can be used to dehydrate because it will be all wrinkled up when it is dried anyway. This is not always true. Produce should be in prime condition. You take from the dehydrator the quality of food you place in the dehydrator. If you select spoiled or severely damaged produce because it is less expensive, you'll be disappointed in the inferior end product. For a high quality product, choose only high quality, mature produce. Of course, the best source of fresh produce is your garden. When planning your garden for dehydration, you should consider:

1. What food you like;
2. What crops you would like to experiment with (We encourage you to dehydrate a little of everything; you won't know what you like until you try it.); and
3. Which varieties are good for dehydrating. In Chapters 4 and 5 we recommend certain varieties of fruits and vegetables. For further details on the best varieties for drying, contact your local agricultural extension service; the telephone number is usually found in the phone book under the heading "County Government."

You can begin your seasonal harvest by drying watercress and chives and end the season with pumpkins and apples. During the "off-season" you can purchase citrus fruits, coconuts, dates, figs, nectarines, papayas, bananas,

Weight Loss Due to Dehydration			
Produce	Amount Purchased or Picked in Pounds	Amount of Dehydrated Product	
		Pounds	Pints
Apples	12	1-1/4	3
Beans, lima	7	1-1/4	2
Beans, snap	6	1/2	2-1/2 1" pieces
Beets	15	1-1/2	3—5
Broccoli	12	1-1/4—1-1/2	12—15
Carrots	15	1-1/4	2—4
Celery	12	3/4	3-1/2—4
Corn	18	2-1/2	4—4-1/2
Greens	3	1/4	5-1/2
Onions	12	1-1/2	11-1/2 sliced 4-1/2 shredded
Peaches	12	1—1-1/2	2—3
Pears	14	1-1/2	3 quartered
Peas	8	3/4	1
Pumpkin	11	3/4	3-1/2
Squash	10	3/4	5
Tomatoes	14	1/2	2-1/2—3

1. Numerous kitchen tools can be used to prepare food for dehydration, though a sharp knife will handle most of the necessary routine cutting tasks.

2. Foods may be chopped or grated before dehydrating for use in soups, stews, or salads.

3. A food processor slices food quickly and uniformly.

4. For making purees, a blender is a must.

or any produce item which is fresh and available from a store. The off-season is a good time to dry leftovers, jerky, or specialty items including fruit and vegetable leathers.

Cutting. Before dehydrating, food must be thoroughly washed; trimmed (soft, spoiled, or unwanted areas removed); sliced; and pretreated if necessary. When cutting food for drying, keep in mind that the larger the cut surface, the faster your food will dry and the better it will retain its nutritive value. Cutting speeds evaporation by exposing more of the food's moisture to the warm, circulating air of the dehydrator. This is why most foods are halved or sliced, rather than left whole, for drying. Cut fruits either with or across the core. Vegetables are diced or cut either crosswise or diagonally, and meats can be sliced either with or across the grain.

Your food should not only be sliced, but sliced *uniformly.* Uneven slicing will cause some pieces to dry faster than others, and all it takes is one moist piece to cause an entire batch to mold. For this reason, you may want to do the majority of your cutting with a slicer or food processor rather than a knife. In fact, you may want to cultivate the habit of slicing food (bananas, tomatoes, etc.) into the same number of slices each time. This greatly simplifies your use of dried food for regular cookbook recipes. For example, if a recipe calls for two bananas and you always cut your bananas into about 20 slices, you would need 40 dried chips for this recipe.

Checking. Nature provides a wax-like coating on the skins of cherries, figs, grapes, prunes, small dark plums, and certain firm berries like blueberries and huckleberries;

however, they all dry better if this waterproofing substance is removed beforehand. The chances of case hardening and rupturing are also reduced if the relatively tough skins of such fruits and berries are cracked minutely in many places; this is called "checking," and it allows internal moisture to be drawn through to the surface and to be evaporated, thus reducing the nutritional loss. These check lines are too fine to be visible.

Because the 30 to 60 seconds required for the de-waxing and checking operation is often too short to let live steam be effective for the contents of the blanching basket, the answer is a very quick dip in briskly boiling water, followed by a dunk in very cold water, and thorough draining.

Length of the dip depends on the relative toughness of the fruits' skins (cranberries are tougher-skinned than currants, for instance). Lay absorbent toweling on the fruit to remove excess moisture from its surface, and continue with the next step in handling the specific fruits.

Pitting. The drying time of fruits with a pit or stone such as cherries can be greatly reduced by pitting them before drying. A cherry pitter makes easy work of this task. Larger pitted fruits such as prunes or apricots should be cut in half to remove the pits. Dehydrating time can be shortened even further by flattening or "popping the backs" of these fruits. Use your thumbs to press the rounded side in. This process exposes more drying surface to the air. To prevent any nutritious juice from dropping to the bottom of the dehydrator, cut each half in half again to give the end product more nutritional value, a brighter color, and faster reconstitution capabilities. Apples and pears may be cored, if desired, before they are dehydrated.

Peeling. Routine peeling of most fruits usually isn't necessary for making a good dried product, but if you feel that you must remove the skins from peaches, and even from apricots and nectarines, simply dip them, a few at a time, in boiling water for 30 to 60 seconds—ample time for firm, ripe fruit. Then cool them quickly in cold water, and pull their skins off by hand.

Most fresh fruits are eaten with the peels on, so this is the way you'll probably want to dry them. Citrus peel, however, is great dried alone and can be candied for a confection. The skins of certain vegetables, though, may become tough when dried; others, like that of the cucumber, take on a bitter taste.

If the fruit has been artificially waxed to help prevent moisture loss, it should definitely be checked to remove the wax. Try fruits both ways, peeled and unpeeled—then decide for yourself.

PRETREATMENT

At one time, pretreating was a standard food drying procedure. However, modern dehydrators have reduced pretreating to the status of an optional measure. The fast drying times and controlled conditions dry food before it has a real chance to spoil; you're dealing with hours of drying time rather than the days involved with older methods. Some authorities single this out to mean that pretreating is a total waste of time; others still maintain that pretreating is essential to properly preserve dried food. Who do you believe? You must master the problem by acting as judge and jury, and decide whether or not to pretreat before drying.

It is true that some foods will keep without pretreating, while others will rapidly deteriorate in color, flavor, texture, and nutrients. Overall, it is reasonable to say that fruits and vegetables do make better dried products if some form of pretreatment is used.

Fruits are normally eaten in the dried state, so appearance is something to consider. Certain ones, like apples, darken to a rusty brown color during drying. Pretreating lessens the browning, while helping to preserve vitamins A and C.

For vegetables, pretreating decreases the chances of deterioration and increases quality and storage life. Furthermore, it serves to inactivate spoilage bacteria. Unblanched vegetables are often tough and strong flavored, whereas pretreated ones are usually tender and tasty—providing that you started with quality produce.

If you believe in keeping food *totally* natural, you'll probably not pretreat. Most pretreatments, with the exceptions of pure steam and natural fruit juice, impart at least some additives to the dried food. Is the slightly longer shelf life or better appearance worth ingesting chemicals?

We've already touched upon the other main argument against pretreating: the speed and efficiency of dehydrators. Many people feel this makes pretreating totally unnecessary and a general waste of time. The final decision to pretreat or not is up to you, the dryer. If you decide to pretreat your dehydrated food, you have a choice of four methods: dipping, blanching, sulfuring, and microwaving.

Dipping

Dipping is a treatment to prevent light colored foods like apricots, bananas, or apples from turning darker (oxidizing when cut fruits are exposed to air). Dipping is primarily used to treat fruit, but can also be used for keeping vegetables, such as potatoes, lighter in color. Anti-oxidants,

To use sodium bisulfite as a dip, soak cut fruit for 2 minutes in a solution of 1 teaspoon bisulfite per quart water.

such as lemon juice, pineapple juice, lime juice, honey, crystalline ascorbic acid (vitamin C); sodium bisulfite; and commercial products containing ascorbic acid, sodium bisulfite, and sugar are effective dipping solutions. When using a dip, drain treated food, rinse thoroughly, and blot off any excess moisture with paper toweling prior to placing the food in the dehydrator.

Sodium Bisulfite.   This compound, when mixed with water to obtain a liquid form of sulfur, is the most effective anti-oxidant—and it's easy to use. Plus for the cost-conscious food dryer, you'll be pleased to know that bisulfite is considerably cheaper to use than either ascorbic acid or citric acid. Use only a food-safe grade of sodium bisulfite that is made for dehydrator use. (*Note*: If subject to sulfur allergic reactions, check with your physician before using sodium bisulfite as a dip.)

To use as a dip with fruit, dissolve 1 teaspoon of bisulfite in 1 quart water and soak the cut fruit for 2 minutes. After the time is up, drain well, rinse lightly, and place the treated fruit on the drying trays. Don't save leftover solution for the next load because it begins to lose its effectiveness as soon as it is exposed to air.

Sodium bisulfite can also be used to *sulfite* fruit. Sulfiting employs stronger concentrations and longer times to reduce oxidation even further. To sulfite, dissolve 1-1/2 to 2 tablespoons of bisulfite in 1 gallon water and soak fruit slices for 5 minutes and halved fruit for 15 minutes. One gallon of solution will treat 20 pounds of fruit. Make sure you lightly rinse the treated fruit in cool water before dehydrating.

Ascorbic Acid.   Ascorbic acid is available in drugstores and health food stores. You can even purchase regular 400 or 500 mg vitamin C tablets and crush them to a powder. (One teaspoon equals 3,000 mg.) Commercial anti-oxidants often contain ascorbic acid, but they don't work nearly as well as pure vitamin C.

Like bisulfite, using ascorbic acid is merely a matter of mixing it with water. Dissolve 1 tablespoon of pure crystalline ascorbic acid in 1 quart cold water. Sliced or chopped food is dipped directly into the solution. When a cup or two of food has accumulated in the container, give it a stir, remove with a slotted spoon, and drain well. Don't leave the food in the solution any longer than 1 hour; holding it longer increases the moisture content and subsequently the drying time. Small quantities of ascorbic acid can also be added to fruit leather puree to maintain its color and increase vitamin C.

Citric Acid.   Citric acid, in crystalline form, is another browning retardant though only one-eighth as effective as ascorbic acid. Pure citric acid crystals can be purchased at a drugstore or at a Kosher food store as "sour salt."

Dissolve 1 tablespoon citric acid in 1 quart water, and treat fruit as described for ascorbic acid. A disadvantage of citric acid is that it can mask the flavor of delicate fruits by giving them a tart taste.

Fruit Juice.   What could be more natural to apply to fruit than fruit juice? Use it as a dip for apples, peaches, and bananas. Stir 1 cup lemon or lime juice into 1 quart lukewarm water; lemon or lime juice contains both ascorbic and citric acids. Dip fruit for no more than 10 minutes, then drain well before drying. Fruit juice is only one-sixth as effective as pure ascorbic acid and has the disadvantage of adding a tart taste to food. *Note:* Pineapple juice can be substituted for lemon or lime juice. Actually, unsweetened pineapple juice usually imparts less flavor to the fruit than either lemon or lime juices.

Honey Dip.   Many dried foods in health food stores have been treated this way. Fruit dipped in honey will be noticeably sweeter, plus it does have more calories so beware if you're watching your waistline.

Dissolve 1 cup sugar in 3 cups hot water. Allow the mixture to cool till lukewarm, then add 1 cup honey. Dip fruit in small batches, remove with a slotted spoon, and drain thoroughly before dehydrating.

Commercial Dips.   Instead of mixing your own dip, you can purchase a commercially prepared anti-oxidant. Most contain ascorbic acid, citric acid, or a combination of the two dissolved in water along with other ingredients. Look for these in supermarkets and use according to the directions on the package.

Blanching

Vegetables with a long cooking time, such as corn, beans, carrots, potatoes, peas, etc., should be blanched to stop the enzyme action that causes flavor loss. Vegetables with a short cooking time, such as zucchini, peppers, onions, mushrooms, or tomatoes, don't require this form of pretreatment. Blanching reduces the number of micro-organisms that cause spoilage in the products, stops destructive chemical changes, preserves the color, stops the ripening process, and generally makes the produce dry faster. The drying is quickened because the outer skin becomes more porous. Blanching process timing must be controlled in order to minimize nutritional losses and destruction of food cells.

1. To water blanch, stir the vegetables into the boiling water. The addition of vinegar will preserve the whiteness of vegetables like cauliflower.

2. When the blanching time is up, remove the vegetables with a slotted spoon. Cool and drain before drying.

Fruits and meats can also be pretreated by blanching; however, blanched fruits may turn soft and hard to handle. Blanching can be done in boiling water or by steam. Several factors may affect blanching times: the amount and types of products, the products' moisture content, and the altitude. When blanching at altitudes over 2000', add an extra 1-1/2 minutes to the times noted on pages 20, 21, and 22.

Water Blanching. When water blanching vegetables, fill your steamer over half full with water, bring to a boil, and stir the vegetables directly into the water. (If you wish, you can make removal easier by putting the vegetables in a wire basket or a cheesecloth wrap.) Be sure to cover the steamer and blanch for the required time.

When vegetables are wilted or heated through, they are ready. Cool in ice water, then blot with paper toweling to remove excess moisture before drying. The water can be saved and reused for other batches.

Steam Blanching. This method of pretreating is preferable to water blanching because fewer water soluble vitamins and minerals are lost. To steam blanch, you'll need a steamer with a lower part that holds water and a perforated upper section that allows steam to circulate. A tight-fitting lid is a must. On short notice, a kettle fitted with a colander will do the trick.

Fill the steamer's lower section with 1-1/2" to 2" of water, and allow to boil. Arrange the vegetables in a thin layer in the upper portion no more than 2" to 3" deep to allow the steam to properly circulate. (The average steamer will hold 2 cups of vegetables.) Place the basket in the steamer, cover tightly, and begin timing. The basket should not touch the water, and the heat should be high enough to keep the water boiling rapidly the entire time. The water can be saved and reused for other batches.

The effects of various pretreatments. Nectarines on the left were syrup blanched, those in the center were sulfited, and the slices on the right were steam blanched.

Pretreating Guide for Fruit		
Suitability for Dehydrating	Fruit	Optional Pretreatment
Excellent	Apples	Dip in citrus fruit juice (pineapple, lemon, etc.) or hold in ascorbic acid or bisulfite dip and then sulfite for approximately 10 minutes or steam blanch 3 to 5 minutes. Rinse in cool water.
	Apricots	Pretreatment is not necessary; however, you can dip in citrus fruit juice or hold cut apricots in ascorbic acid or bisulfite dip. Steam blanch 2 to 4 minutes or syrup blanch.
	Bananas	Honey dip for crisper slices. Bananas may be sprinkled with fruit flavored gelatin powder or lemon juice.
	Cherries	None
	Citrus Peel	None
	Coconut	None
	Dates	None
	Figs	None
	Grapes	None
	Nectarines	Pretreatment is not necessary; however, you can dip in citrus juice or sulfite for 10 to 15 minutes, then rinse in cold water.
	Peaches	Pretreatment is not necessary; however, you can dip in citrus juice or hold peaches in ascorbic acid or bisulfite dip, then sulfite 5 to 15 minutes. Rinse in cool water.
	Pears	Pretreatment is not necessary; however, you can dip in citrus juice or hold in ascorbic acid or bisulfite, then sulfite for 5 to 15 minutes. Rinse in cool water.
	Pineapples	None
	Prune Plums	None
Good	Currants	None
	Papaya	None
	Plums	None
	Rhubarb	Steam blanch for 1 to 2 minutes until tender or use a honey dip.
Fair	Blueberries	None
	Kiwi	None
	Persimmons	None
Poor	Avocados	None
	Berries (blackberries, boysenberries, cranberries, huckleberries, raspberries)	None
	Citrus Fruits	None
	Melons	None

Pretreating Guide for Vegetables		
Suitability for Dehydrating	**Vegetable**	**Optional Pretreatment**
Excellent	Onions	None
	Peppers, Hot/Chili	None
Good	Beans, Green and Wax	Water blanch 3 to 4 minutes, or steam blanch 4 to 6 minutes over water; you may use 1 teaspoon sodium bisulfite per cup water. For a more tender product, freeze the blanched beans for approximately 30 minutes before drying.
	Beets	None
	Carrots	Steam blanch 3 to 4 minutes over water; you may use 1 teaspoon sodium bisulfite per cup water. You may also dip steamed carrots in a cornstarch solution, 1 tablespoon cornstarch per cup water, and drain before placing on trays; however, this is not necessary.
	Corn	You may use 1 teaspoon sodium bisulfite per cup water to steaming solution. Steam blanch 1 to 3 minutes.
	Mushrooms	Pretreatment is not necessary; however, you can steam blanch 2 to 3 minutes over water. You may use 1 teaspoon sodium bisulfite per cup water.
	Okra	Water blanch 2 to 3 minutes, or steam blanch 4 to 5 minutes.
	Parsnips	Water blanch 2 to 3 minutes, or steam blanch 3 to 5 minutes.
	Peas	Steam blanch 3 minutes until indented, rinse in cold water, and blot with a paper towel. Or, soak for 2 minutes in a solution of 1 teaspoon sodium bisulfite per cup water.
	Peppers, Green or Red	Pretreatment is not necessary; however, you can soak in 1 teaspoon sodium bisulfite per cup water.
	Popcorn	None
	Potatoes	Steam blanch 4 to 6 minutes; you may use 1 teaspoon sodium bisulfite per cup water to steaming solution.
	Pumpkin	None
	Rutabagas	Water blanch 2 to 3 minutes, or steam blanch 3 to 5 minutes.
	Tomatoes	None
	Turnips	Water blanch 3 to 5 minutes, or steam blanch 5 to 8 minutes.
Fair	Artichokes	Water blanch 2 to 4 minutes, or steam blanch 3 to 5 minutes.
	Asparagus	Water blanch 2 to 3 minutes, or steam blanch 3 to 5 minutes.
	Beans, Lima	Water blanch 2 to 3 minutes, or steam blanch 2 to 4 minutes.
	Broccoli	Water blanch 2 to 3 minutes, or steam blanch 3 to 5 minutes.
	Cabbage	Steam blanch 2 to 3 minutes over water; you may use 1 teaspoon sodium bisulfite per cup water.
	Eggplant	Pretreatment is not necessary; however, you can steam blanch 3 to 5 minutes over water; you may use 1 teaspoon sodium bisulfite per cup water.
	Kohlrabi	Water blanch 3 to 5 minutes, or steam blanch 5 to 8 minutes.
	Peas, Black-Eyed	None

Pretreating Guide for Vegetables (continued)		
Suitability for Dehydrating	Vegetable	Optional Pretreatment
Fair	Squash, Summer	Steam blanch 2 to 3 minutes.
	Sweet Potatoes (Yams)	Steam blanch 2 to 3 minutes until almost tender.
	Zucchini	Steam blanch 2 to 3 minutes. Do not steam slices meant for use as chips.
Poor	Brussels Sprouts	Water blanch 3 to 5 minutes, or steam blanch 6 to 7 minutes.
	Cauliflower	Steam blanch 5 minutes, or water blanch 3 to 4 minutes in a vinegar solution of 1 tablespoon vinegar per gallon water.
	Celery	Steam blanch 2 to 3 minutes, or water blanch 30 seconds to 1 minute in a baking soda solution of 1 teaspoon baking soda per cup water.
	Cucumber	None
	Greens	Pretreatment is not necessary; however, you can steam blanch until slightly wilted.
	Kale	Pretreatment is not necessary; however, you can steam blanch until wilted.
	Lettuce	Pretreatment is not necessary; however, you can steam blanch until wilted.
	Radishes	None
	Spinach	Pretreatment is not necessary; however, you can steam blanch until wilted.
	Squash, Winter	None
	Swiss Chard	Water blanch 2 minutes, or steam blanch for 2 to 3 minutes.

Syrup Blanching. Syrup blanching is sometimes used to pretreat fruits such as apples, figs, nectarines, peaches, pears, plums, and prunes. If desired, hold the cut fruit in one of the dipping solutions while preparing the syrup. Combine 2 cups white corn syrup, 2 cups sugar, and 4 cups water in a large saucepan. When the mixture begins to boil, add the fruit and simmer for 8 to 10 minutes. Take the pan off the burner and allow the fruit to stand in the syrup an additional 20 to 30 minutes, according to the size of the slices. (If allowed to remain in the syrup too long, the fruit will become mushy.) Drain, rinse if desired, and then dehydrate. The syrup can be saved for reuse until the next batch.

Sulfuring

This pretreatment method is *not* recommended for use with a dehydrator indoors; the fumes produced are very irritating and may be harmful to one's health.

Microwaving

A relatively new method of pretreating vegetables is to heat them in a microwave oven. Place the vegetables one layer deep in a microwave-safe dish and process for three-fourths the time required to completely cook them when fresh. Stir when halfway along to get a more even treatment. When the vegetables are done, remove them, place on the dehydrator trays, and load immediately in the dryer.

Again with this method, you are cooking the vegetables and their flavor will reflect that.

Experiment with both treated and untreated food in your storage to see which will best suit your needs. Remember, proper storage is critical to the quality of the stored product whether treated or untreated.

DRYING _____

The dehydrator should be operated in a well ventilated room so that water vapor will be carried away. Load the trays with prepared food a single layer deep. Different kinds of fruits and vegetables may be dried at the same time, but odorous vegetables, such as onions, should be dried separately.

Before placing the trays in the dehydrator, preheat the unit. Since the moisture content of the food will cause an initial temperature drop in the dehydrator, start drying 5° to 10° higher than the recommended or normal drying temperature. After an hour or so, lower the temperature back to the normal drying temperature. Remember, *be sure to turn the temperature back.*

Set the temperature carefully, keeping in mind that the temperature should be high enough to evaporate moisture from the food but not cook it. Food should be dried as rapidly as possible, yet not so fast that case hardening occurs. Actually, *case hardening takes place when the temperature cooks the outside of the food and traps the moisture in the center.* The moisture can't escape and will cause a flat, sour taste; the product then must be discarded. Generally, you can adhere to the following settings:

Herbs	95°F
Raising Bread	110°F
Making Yogurt	115°F
Vegetables	125°F
Fruits	135°F
Leathers, Fruit Rolls	135°F
Meat and Fish	145°F
Jerky	145°F

When doing fruits and vegetables together, a compromise setting of 130°F is acceptable because the moist fruit will prevent the vegetables from case hardening. You may wish to experiment with temperatures that are 10° to 15° lower than those suggested in the book. For some foods this will result not only in a better looking, higher quality product, but also a longer drying time (i.e., pineapple may be dried as low as 100°F) with superior results. This does *not* apply to meats, fish, fowl, or dairy products.

Examine the food from time to time to check for dryness. You may want to rotate the trays 180° halfway through the drying cycle to save energy and reduce drying time.

How Long Does Food Drying Take?

There are several variable factors that help determine the time it takes to dehydrate various foods. They include:

1. *The humidity in the air.* Air must be kept in motion. Stagnant air soon takes on as much moisture as it can hold, then drying no longer takes place. Drying must be a continuous process so growth of microorganisms is prevented. If the air contains 60% humidity rather than 90% humidity, food will dry in a shorter period of time. To help you determine the amount of humidity at various times of the year and in different parts of our country, we have included typical percentage humidity maps on pages 24 and 25.

2. *The amount of water in the food.* Various foods differ in moisture content. For example, on the average, tomatoes contain 94% water. According to the United States Department of Agriculture, the amount of water in a food will depend on the growing season, rainfall, and other environmental factors.

3. *The size and thickness of the cut piece of food.* Food cut 1/4″ thick will dry faster than that cut 3/4″ thick. Uniform size pieces of food, spread evenly in single layers, give the best result.

4. *The quality of the electric dehydrator.* The more efficient the dehydrator, the less time food will take to dehydrate and the more nutritious it will be. One of the most important factors is the heat/air balance; the airflow must be correct for the amount of heat being supplied to the trays within the dehydrator. The heat should be controlled by an adjustable thermostat, and the air circulation must be such that moisture-saturated air is constantly replaced by dry air to keep the dehydration process continuous.

These factors and guidelines are important to have some control over how long food will take to dehydrate. Times may vary greatly from one area of the country to another or even from day to day. Keep records of your specific experiences for future references. Further details on drying times are given in Chapters 4 through 8.

JANUARY

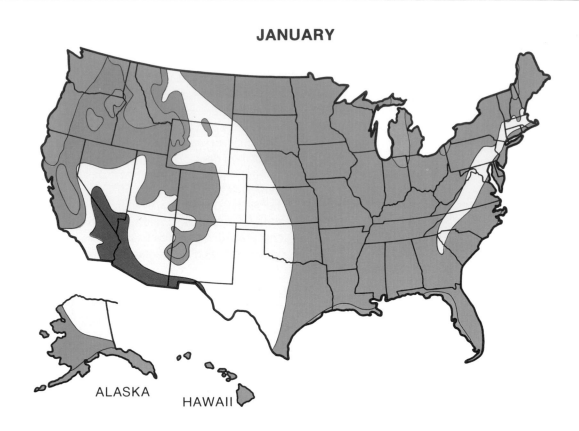

APRIL

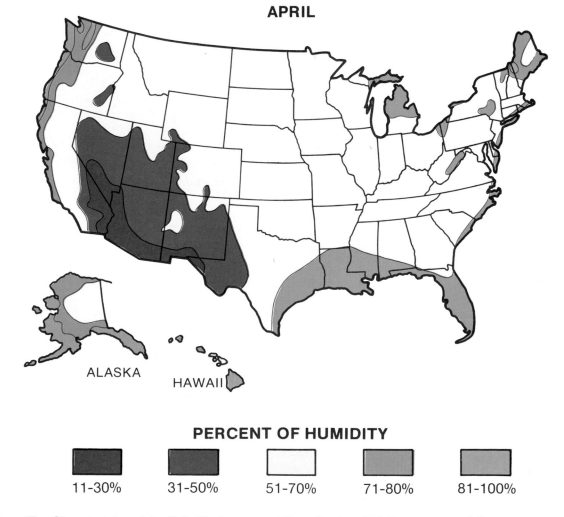

PERCENT OF HUMIDITY

| 11-30% | 31-50% | 51-70% | 71-80% | 81-100% |

Courtesy: The Climatic Atlas of the U.S., Environmental Data Service, U.S. Department of Commerce.

JULY

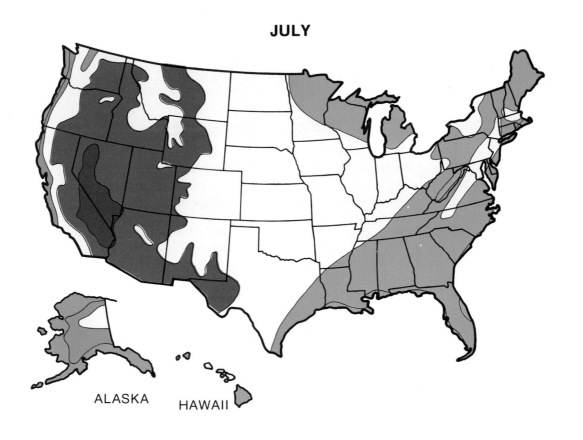

ALASKA   HAWAII

OCTOBER

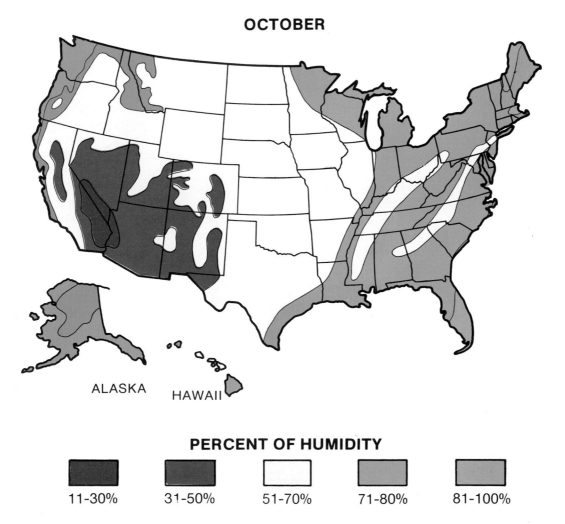

ALASKA   HAWAII

PERCENT OF HUMIDITY

| 11-30% | 31-50% | 51-70% | 71-80% | 81-100% |

TESTING

Food should be dry enough to prevent microbacterial growth and subsequent spoilage. The safe *maximum* percentages of water remaining in home dried produce are no more than 10% for vegetables and no more than 20% for fruits. Note the word *maximum*; most experts feel for best storage that the percentage of moisture (residual moisture) should be as follows: fruits, 10%; vegetables, 5%; grains, 10 to 12%; and meats, 20%. Commercially dried fruits often contain more water—especially when they're "tenderized"—but they also may contain additives other than simple sulfur dioxide to protect against spoilage from the higher content of moisture. Because we don't have the food industry's highly refined means of testing for and controlling moisture, we must count on experience and testing to tell us whether the food is dry or not.

Testing is achieved through look, feel, and taste. Remove several pieces of food from the dehydrator trays and allow them to cool. When cut through the center, there should be no visible signs of moisture. A darker, wet interior indicates the need for extended dehydration. Usually it is better to overdry than to underdry. When in doubt continue drying for additional time.

Fruit generally can be considered adequately dry when no moisture can be squeezed from a piece of it when cut; when it has become rather tough and pliable; and when a few pieces squeezed together fall apart when the pressure is released. Leathery, suede-like, and springy are descriptions you'll see in the individual instructions for fruits. Several others, such as figs and cherries, also are slightly "sticky."

Vegetables are generally "brittle" or "tough to brittle" when they're dry enough; corn and peas will shatter when hit with a hammer. A few vegetables like tomatoes are leathery to the touch.

Another way to determine dryness is by weighing the vegetables and fruits before and after dehydrating to ensure that the proper amount of moisture has been removed. The following example assumes you are dehydrating 10 pounds of onions that have a moisture content of 89% or .89, its decimal equivalent.

1. After removing peels and other waste parts, determine the total weight of the water in the fresh vegetables.
   Total pounds fresh vegetables × % water content =
   Total pounds water
   10 pounds × .89 = 8.9 pounds water
2. Compute the pounds of water to be removed during dehydration. Vegetables can only contain a maximum of 5% moisture, so 95%, or .95, of the water must be taken out. (Fruits should contain 10 to 20% moisture, so 80 to 90%—or .80 to .90—of the water must be removed.)
   Total pounds water × .95 =
   Total pounds water to be removed
   8.9 pounds × .95 = 8.46 pounds water removed

3. Lastly, find the proper weight of the vegetables after dehydrating.
   Total pounds fresh vegetables -
   Total pounds water to be removed =
   Total pounds of dried vegetables
   10 pounds - 8.46 pounds = 1.54 pounds

In other words, after dehydration your onions should weigh only 1-1/2 pounds. Weights higher than those recommended indicate that too much moisture remains and the vegetables (fruits) could mold. Return them to the dehydrator for more time, then reweigh.

Meats and all protein foods should be *very* dry unless they are to be refrigerated or frozen for long time storage. Meat is sufficiently dried when it is dark in color, fibrous, and forms sharp points when bent.

Herbs are thoroughly dried when brittle. Their leaves shatter when rubbed together. Further information on testing dehydrated food is given in Chapters 4 to 8.

PACKAGING AND STORAGE

All your work will go to waste unless you package and store the dehydrated food properly. While it's true that dehydrating considerably extends the shelf life of food, it cannot protect it from insects, other pests, air, light, and moisture. However, proper post-dehydrating care will preserve the quality of the food and lengthen its life-span.

Packaging

Any container that has been employed for food storage previously is safe to use for storing dehydrated food. It should have a firm shape and must have a tight-fitting lid. There is no need to purchase special containers; recycle old ones. For instance, recycled glass, salad dressing, peanut butter, pickle, mustard, and canning jars are good and will permit you to see the food. (Dark glass jars are considered best for certain dried foods such as herbs and fruits because the light won't be able to fade them or affect their nutrients or quality.) Potato chip, shortening, and metal coffee cans with tight-fitting plastic lids also make good containers for storage. But, when storing in a metal can it's wise to put a plastic bag in the can to keep the food from touching the metal. Containers such as these can be sealed tightly by wrapping the joining area with plasticized pressure-sensitive tape.

Before using any container for the storage of dehydrated foods, clean, scald, and thoroughly dry the container. Also make sure that the food has *completely* cooled. Packaging warm is a definite "don't." Heat causes sweat, or condensation, to form on the inside of the container which will eventually result in the food molding or spoiling. But *do* package the food as soon as it is cool to prevent any moisture from being reabsorbed. It is permissible to leave the food in the dehydrator to cool. But make sure the door is closed and the unit is turned off. In 30 minutes to an hour, transfer the food into proper storage containers. Leaving the food in the dehydrator too long after the food is dry will cause humidity from the air to collect on it and make it sticky.

Pack the dehydrated food without crushing. Small containers are better than large ones as some moisture from the air will be absorbed each time the container is opened. Try to use a container size that will hold enough food that it can be used up in a relatively short time. In fact, for easier use, package your dehydrated food in meal- or snack-size portions; every time you open up a large container, the food is exposed to air, resulting in additional vitamin loss. Small portions will also prevent the entire batch from being ruined if one piece spoils.

Heavy-duty "zip-lock" or "self-sealing" plastic bags, as well as those that must be sealed by machine, are excellent for dehydrated foods. Squeezing the pouch tightly against the food it contains will effectively void the air just prior to sealing the plastic bag. This ensures a good air-free storage environment inside the plastic container. Care must be taken in selecting a bag sealer to find a unit that creates a wide, leak-proof seal. The seals on most units are 1/32" to 1/16" thick and often prove inadequate. Look for a seal that is no less than 3/8" thick; the thicker the better.

When vegetables are dried they should have no more than 10% moisture content. Fruits may have 10 to 20% moisture content. If fruits and vegetables are going to be stored in the same large container, it is suggested that they be sealed separately in airtight plastic bags to prevent moisture equalization that tends to mold the vegetables.

To further protect the food from moisture, a small muslin bag containing about 1/2 cup of silica gel—a chemical which absorbs moisture from the air—can be put in with the sealed container of food. Silica gel is readily available in hobby stores and florist shops. Thoroughly seal the dehydrated food in individual plastic bags before putting it in the container with the silica gel. While it's not toxic, silica gel should not come in direct contact with the food since the gel is not fit for human consumption. Check the silica occasionally. If the crystals have changed from white to light pink they are saturated with moisture. Remove the crystals from the muslin bag, spread them out on the tray, and dry them in the dehydrator at 140°F until they have again turned white. The silica gel can be used time and again.

Labeling your dehydrated food containers not only makes them more attractive, but also allows you to keep a check on the age of the food inside. Basically, all you need on the label is the contents and the drying date. But it is also a good idea to include on the label drying time, weight of produce before and after drying, and humidity at the time of drying; this information will be helpful in improving your dehydrating techniques. In addition, many dryers put such data on the label as the number of servings in the package or container and—for the more involved dishes—directions for preparing the food. While this information may be printed on a piece of masking tape, why settle for plain? Look in stationary and office supply stores to see what they have to offer in terms of decorative labels, stickers, and decals. Look for ones with old fashioned pictures or "From the Kitchen of..." for a personal touch, or purchase plain labels and create your own design. The labels can be glued to the containers, attached with decorative tape, or pasted on with stickers.

Storage

Ideally, dehydrated food should be stored in a cool, dark, dry location. Food held in storage at 50° to 60°F retains more food value than when it is stored at higher temperatures. The absence of light in the storage area preserves colors and vitamins. For your dehydrated food storage location, try to pick a spot where these conditions don't vary too widely. Basements often meet the criteria, but be on the lookout for insects and other pests that could contaminate your stocks.

Should you suspect contamination, it's possible to *pasteurize* your dehydrated food by placing it in the oven at 175°F for 15 minutes. Another method of protection is to subject the food to 0°F in the deep freeze for 48 hours to kill any larvae that may be on it. It is then safe with either method to store it on the shelf in an insectproof container.

Check for moisture in storage containers several times the first week after the food has been dried. If moisture appears on the inside of the storage container when the contents are shook, put the food back into the dehydrator and dry for a longer period of time. Use your supply of dehydrated food on a first in, first out basis. Put new containers to the rear of your storage shelves and move older ones forward.

Don't place dehydrated food storage containers directly on a concrete floor. If shelves can't be constructed, run long 2″ by 4″ pieces of lumber on the floor, so that the cans or similar containers have air under them. Never place storage containers flush against a concrete wall. Leave a small amount of air space.

Dehydrated food may be kept from year to year. It will have higher nutritional value if you only try to store each year's harvest to carry over until the next year's supply is available. If you have some food left, do not discard it but go ahead and use it unless you can obviously see that it doesn't have quality.

This attractive dried soup mix tastes just as good as it looks. By combining dried ingredients ahead of time, a delicious cup of soup can be ready in just minutes.

RECONSTITUTING DEHYDRATED FOOD

Rehydration is the process of restoring liquid to dehydrated food. This reconstitution or refreshment is an important part in learning how to use dehydrated food. Of course, not all dehydrated food requires rehydration. Dried fruits and fruit leathers make a delicious snack when eaten dry, as does meat jerky. Dried vegetables can be eaten as chips with various dips; or they can be powdered, flaked, shredded, or chopped and added to soups, stews, and similar dishes. Herbs can also be added to other foods without rehydrating.

Properly dried foods refresh well. They return practically to their original size, form, and appearance. If carefully handled, they will retain much of their aroma and flavor as well as the minerals and appreciable amounts of vitamins.

There are several methods of reconstituting dehydrated food, including soaking in water, placing in boiling water, and cooking. It's important to remember, however, not to add salt or sugar to the water during the initial 5 minutes of reconstitution as they hinder the absorption process.

Soaking. As a general rule, the amount of water or other liquid used in reconstitution is 2 cups of food per 1 cup of liquid. If necessary, gradually add more liquid until the desired texture is obtained and the food won't absorb any additional liquid. Keep in mind when rehydrating to use only enough water for soaking as the food will absorb. Over-soaking produces a loss of flavor and sometimes a mushy, water-logged product.

Fruits can be soaked in water, cider, various fruit juices, yogurt, cordials, or fruit liqueurs until they reabsorb most of the liquid that was originally taken from them. This may be accomplished by placing the slices of dried produce in a shallow container, covering them with a thin layer of liquid, and then laying a towel over the top (the towel is optional). Using this method, fruit will usually plump up within 1 to 2 hours, but overnight soaking may be necessary for large or whole pieces of dried food. Overnight soaking should be done in the refrigerator.

To soften fruit for snacks, place a cup of fruit into a zip-lock plastic bag with 2 or 3 drops of water and put it into the refrigerator overnight. Unless the fruit will be used within 2 or 3 days, it should be kept refrigerated.

Vegetables can be soaked in water, consommé bouillon, vegetable juices, or milk (refrigerate) and will usually rehydrate within 1 or 2 hours. But depending on the size of the dried food pieces and the degree to which the pieces have been dried, rehydration may take as long as 8 hours. Generally speaking, rehydration is somewhat proportional to dehydration. That is, those food pieces that take the longest to dehydrate will take the longest to rehydrate. As you dehydrate foods take note of the slow ones, then you'll be able to allow extra time for rehydration.

When reconstituting dehydrated food, save the liquid employed and try to find another use for it: use as a fruit or vegetable juice; substitute the rehydration liquid for a different liquid called for in recipes; add to soups or stews; save to use for rehydrating other foods; or freeze for use in soups, leathers, pies, or compotes. Rehydration liquid has great nutritional value—don't pour it down the drain.

Boiling Water. Place 1 cup of vegetables into 1 cup of boiling water and soak for 5 to 20 minutes. Then prepare as desired: simmer, place in casseroles, etc. To reconstitute fruits for pie, place 1 cup of water and 1 cup of fruit into a pan and simmer until tender. If the pie is to be thickened, it may require more moisture. Don't add a lot of moisture in the beginning and cause it to be too thin. It is easy to see if more water is necessary for the fruit to plump up.

To soften fruit for use in cookies, candy, or cakes, place in a steamer with 1″ of water in the bottom and let it steam

for 3 minutes. Use kitchen shears to cut the fruit into bite-size pieces.

Cooking. The final method of rehydration—cooking—is the simplest and fastest. Fruits and vegetables can be cooked in water, broths, or juices or added directly to soups and stews to which extra liquid has been incorporated. Dried food can be cooked by three basic methods: stovetop, slow cooker, and microwave oven.

When cooking dried food on a stovetop, the amount of liquid needed for cooking/rehydrating will vary somewhat according to how the food will be used. For fruits and vegetables to be used in soufflés, pies, quick breads, doughs, and batters, add two parts liquid to three parts dried food. Use one part liquid to one part dried food for vegetable side dishes, fruit toppings, or compotes. (*Note:* More water may be added during the cooking time if the food appears too dry.)

Once the amount of liquid has been determined, you can begin cooking/rehydrating. To cook dried fruits on the stovetop, add the fruit to the appropriate amount of boiling water. Turn down the heat and simmer the fruit for 10 to 15 minutes or until tender. Rehydrated cooked fruits are sweeter than fresh fruits, so govern the inclusion of sweetening agents accordingly. With dried vegetables, place them in a pan containing the correct amount of liquid and bring it to a boil. Reduce the heat, and allow the vegetables to simmer until tender.

For the two other cooking options—the slow cooker and the microwave—use the same liquid amounts as recommended for stovetop cooking. With a slow cooker, place the dehydrated food and liquid in the unit. Cover and cook for several hours on low until the food is rehydrated and tender. In a microwave, place the food and liquid in a glass dish, cover, and cook for 2 to 10 minutes on full power until the food rehydrates. Stir occasionally. Thorough cooking may require a longer time.

When using the stovetop or microwave methods, do not add salt, spices, sugar, or sweeteners until the end of the cooking time; otherwise, they will hinder the rehydration process.

When substituting dehydrated vegetables or fruit in recipes that call for fresh produce, only rehydrate as much of the vegetables or fruit as is needed. In most recipes, you need only substitute 1/2 to 2/3 cup of dry vegetables for 1 cup of fresh vegetables. Other dry equivalents are given in the table below.

Fresh Produce	Dry Equivalents
1 onion	1-1/2 tablespoons onion powder
	1/4 cup dried minced onions
1 green pepper	1/4 cup green pepper flakes
1 cup carrots	4 tablespoons powdered carrots
	1/2 cup (heaped) dried carrots
1 cup spinach	2 to 3 tablespoons powdered spinach
1 medium tomato	1 tablespoon powdered tomato
1/2 cup (approx.) tomato puree	1 tablespoon powdered tomato
20 pounds tomatoes	18 ounces dried sliced tomatoes

In recipes that specify quantities (fresh or dried) in ounces, use these equivalent volume measurements:

1 ounce = 1/8 cup = 2 tablespoons
2 ounces = 1/4 cup = 4 tablespoons
8 ounces = 1 cup = 16 tablespoons

Remember that many dried foods taste and resemble their fresh counterparts after reconstitution. But dried foods are unique and shouldn't be expected to resemble a fresh product in every respect. Reconstituted tomatoes, for example, do not look like fresh tomatoes in a salad, but they will make excellent tomato sauce or can be pulverized to make fine tomato paste. Be creative and resourceful; an amazing number of new and interesting recipes awaits you.

When dehydrated and then reduced to a powder, these 15 whole tomatoes will fit in this small jar.

4

DEHYDRATING FRUITS

You'll have fun drying fruit; it's one of the oldest and most popular dehydrated foods. Enjoy dried fruit as a naturally sweet snack, in your favorite recipes, candied, or in good tasting leathers. Apples, peaches, bananas, and pears are long-time dehydrating favorites. But why stick to the tried and true? Dare to dry dates, have a fling with figs, or perk yourself up with persimmons. Challenge yourself to master them all!

GENERAL RULES FOR DEHYDRATING FRUITS

The basic steps of dehydrating have been covered in the previous chapter. But, before we take a look at specific dehydrating techniques for specific fruits, let's review some of the important points of drying fruits.

Preparation and Pretreatment. For a high quality end product, choose only a high quality, mature fruit. When fruits are mature their natural sugar content is high as is the nutritional content. Remove the moisture quickly to prevent spoilage. Use only firm fruit to dry into slices. Overripe and bruised fruits may turn black and look burnt. Bananas are also best when the fruit has brown speckles on the peel. When the skin has turned black, the banana may be pureed for leather or used to make good banana bread.

If fruits (or vegetables) are to be dried with skins on, they should be washed thoroughly. In all likelihood, many of them have been commercially waxed or sprayed if purchased at a market. Most waxes and sprays can be removed by washing in a biodegradable cleaner or a vinegar water solution and then rinsing in clear water. If, however, the wax or spray cannot be removed, then it would be wiser to peel before drying. (Some fruits, like grapes and certain berries, have a natural wax coating that must be removed by checking. See Chapter 3 for checking instructions.) Since quality begins to deteriorate the minute you start washing, prepare only as much fruit as you can dry at one time.

Uniform slicing can make a big difference in how evenly your fruit dries; pieces of differing thickness will require varied drying times. In addition, keep in mind that the smaller you make the slices, the faster the drying time and the better the quality. Small fruits, like berries, can be left whole, but larger ones should be halved, sliced, or diced. Trim away any unavoidable bruised areas.

There are pros and cons for peeling. As mentioned earlier, try fruits both ways to find the method you prefer. There are many ways to pretreat fruit. They are discussed in the pretreatment section in Chapter 3. Here again it is a matter of individual preference. The only way to discover the method you like best is to try different ways.

Dehydrating

Most fruits do not have strong odors, so feel free to dry them together. What odors do exist are kept from mixing by the horizontal airflow of quality dehydrators. Arrange the fruit in a *single layer* on the drying trays, leaving some space between pieces for better air circulation. The skin side (if left on) should be down to prevent juice from dripping. Small berries should be stirred occasionally to promote uniform drying. Do not add fresh fruit to a batch that is nearly dry; the increased humidity will cause the partially dried food to reabsorb moisture and possibly spoil. For exact instructions, refer to the fruit dehydrating guide. Remember: Your times may vary considerably from those listed.

Testing

Since dried fruits are generally eaten without being rehydrated, they should not be dehydrated to the point of brittleness. Most fruits should have a 10 to 20% moisture content when dried.

Cool several pieces of fruit and test for dryness. Cut the pieces in half; there should be no visible moisture. Now feel and taste—they should be anywhere from pliable to brittle depending on the particular fruit. It's better to have the fruit a little too dry than to have it too moist and run the risk of molding. When you are satisfied that the fruit is dry, cool it in the dehydrator or in a bowl for 30 minutes to 1 hour, and then remove and package.

Rehydrating

There may be times when you'll want to rehydrate your dried fruit before eating. Let the dried fruit stand in just enough boiling water to cover it; too much water can result in vitamin and mineral losses. The fruit should be ready in approximately 7 minutes or when most of the water has been absorbed. Dried fruit can also be rehydrated by sprinkling it with water or fruit juice and letting it stand. If the rehydrated fruit is not to be used immediately, refrigerate it to prevent spoilage.

Another alternative is to cook the dried fruit in water or fruit juice. Add the fruit to boiling water and simmer for 10 to 15 minutes. Because spices and sweeteners will hinder rehydration, don't add them until the fruit is nearly done. When substituting dried fruit in your own recipes, 1/2 cup dehydrated is generally equivalent to 1 cup fresh.

FRUIT DEHYDRATING GUIDE ─────────

Here are step-by-step instructions for drying all the popular fruits. They're arranged in terms of drying suitability: excellent, good, fair, and poor. If you're a beginner, you might want to stick to those rated "excellent" until you gain some experience.

As far as dehydrating times are concerned, the ones given in the step-by-step instructions are *approximations only*. Because there are so many variables, exact times are impossible to estimate. Keep this in mind and you'll avoid a great deal of frustration. However, as a general guide for judging drying in your region of the country, consult the humidity maps found on pages 24 and 25. Find the color that corresponds to your area for the season in which you are dehydrating. Now match that color with the appropriate color square alongside each fruit listing for a more accurate approximation. If you prefer your fruit pretreated, refer to the pretreating guide on page 20.

EXCELLENT FOR DEHYDRATING ─────────

Apples    hrs

Mature apples, fresh and undamaged, are the type you'll want to dry. Winesap, Jonathan, Granny Smith, Pippin, Rome Beauty, McIntosh Red, and Baldwin are all excellent varieties.

Step-by-Step
1. Wash, pare, and core the apples. Or wash and just remove the seeds. Peelers, corers, and a slicer will make your work a good deal easier.
2. Cut the apples into 1/4" to 3/8" slices or rings; discard any bruised portions.
3. Dry at 135°F until pliable. For a sweeter flavor, sprinkle the slices with sugar and cinnamon prior to drying.

Note: Dehydrated apples lend themselves particularly well for use in a variety of baked goods such as pies, tea breads, and cookies.

Apricots    hrs

For the best results when dehydrating, avoid apricots that are hard or unripe. Pick ones that are nearly round with yellow to orange skin and flesh, depending on the variety. Try Manchu, Tilton, Moongold, Goldcot, or Blenheim/Royal varieties.

Step-by-Step
1. Wash the apricots, cut in half, slice, and remove the pits or stones.
2. Dehydrate the apricots at 135°F until pliable.

Note: Dried and rehydrated apricots pep up meat dishes, salads, fruitcake, pies, candy, or cookies. Puree them to make an appetizing apricot sauce.

Bananas   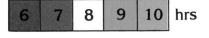 hrs

Bananas are one of the quickest and easiest fruits to dry, as well as one of the tastiest. Large yellow varieties, like Cavandish or Martinique, dehydrate best. Those that are all yellow or lightly brown specked will be the sweetest; avoid green or overripe bananas.

Step-by-Step
1. Peel the bananas and cut into 1/8" to 1/4" slices. (Cut away any bruised portions.)
2. Dehydrate bananas at 135°F until leathery.

Note: Consume this tropical fruit dry as a snack; in trail mixes, cookies, cakes, and breads; or on cereals. Fried, they make scrumptious fritters.

Coconut  **hrs**

Choose coconuts that are fresh and heavy for their size. Moldy or wet areas indicate age. The coconut should be full of fluid or milk; shake the fruit to test.

Step-by-Step

1. Puncture one end of the coconut and pour out the sweet milk, which can be consumed or used in cooking.
2. Using a hammer, crack the fruit around the middle of the hard, stoney shell.
3. Steam the broken coconut for 30 seconds to 1 minute or simply gouge out the meat with a knife.
4. Remove the dark outer skin, and grate the meat.
5. Dry at 135°F until leathery and crisp.

Note: Dehydrated coconut is extremely versatile. Incorporate it in cakes, icings, pudding, pies, and granola, or use as an all-around topping.

Cherries  **hrs**

Several varieties of cherries are suitable for dehydrating. For instance, sweet cherries such as Bing, Lambert, Napoleon, Royal Anne, and Van are very tasty when dried. If you intend to dehydrate a sour variety such as Meteor or Montmorency, reserve them after drying for cooking. Pick extra firm, juicy, meaty cherries.

Step-by-Step

1. Wash the cherries, cut in half, and remove stems and pits. Cherries can be dried whole, but the drying time will be considerably longer and the quality reduced. A cherry pitter is a boon to preparation.
2. Place cherry halves on the trays skin-side down. Start dehydrating at 145°F for approximately 2 hours; then reduce the temperature to 135°F for the remainder of the drying time.
3. Dehydrate the cherries until leathery, sticky, and raisin-like. Watch the cherries closely toward the end of the time to prevent overdrying.

Note: Dried sweet cherries make a raisin-like snack treat and can be substituted for raisins in cookies, cakes, and breads. Use sour cherries rehydrated in cobblers, crisps, and pies.

Dates 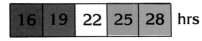  **hrs**

Dates are a chief source of food in the Middle East as well as North Africa. Select large, bright red dates or the smaller, sweeter dark ones for drying.

Step-by-Step

1. Wash the dates well. Cut in half and pit if desired.
2. Dehydrate dates at 135°F until leathery.

Note: Dates can be eaten dry as a snack, either plain or cut up and rolled in confectioner's sugar. They can also be added to cereals, fruitcakes, cookies, and trail mixes.

Citrus Peel  **hrs**

Citrus peel is excellent when dried. When selecting fruit for peel, make sure it shows no signs of mold, decay, or especially of being dyed, color-treated, or sprayed.

Step-by-Step

1. Wash the skins thoroughly to remove any dirt. To remove wax or sprays, wash in biodegradable cleaner or vinegar water and rinse well.
2. Peel off just the very top layer of skin which holds the flavoring oils; the remaining white material is too bitter for use.
3. Peels can be candied.
4. Dehydrate at 135°F until crisp.

Note: Cut citrus peel in strips to store. Grate or chop when needed for fruitcakes, puddings, and candies.

Figs  hrs

Figs are naturally sweet and rich in calcium and phosphorus. Ripe figs will have a brownish-maroon skin and pinkish flesh. Brown Turkey, Black Mission, and White Adriatic are all excellent when dried.

Step-by-Step
1. Wash figs, remove their stems, and cut out any blemishes.
2. Quarter large figs and spread one layer deep on the drying trays with the skin-side down. Figs can also be dried whole, but they will take considerably longer to dehydrate and must first be checked.
3. Dry at 135°F until pliable.

Note: Dried figs are tasty as a confection, stuffed, in fig bars or fig newtons, or in cake and bread recipes. Rehydrated, they can be incorporated into compotes and fruit salads.

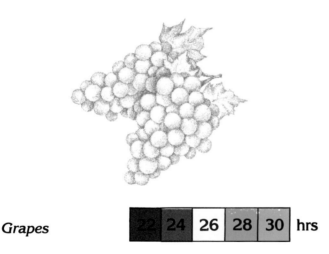

Grapes

Dehydrated grapes have their own unique name—raisins. Green Thompson or black seedless are the best drying grapes. Muscats also make excellent raisins, although they have seeds that must be removed by hand—a very time-consuming process.

Step-by-Step
1. Wash and remove the stems from the grapes, leaving the fruits whole.
2. "Check" for 30 to 90 seconds in boiling water to reduce drying time.
3. Dry at 135°F until wrinkled and pliable. Dehydrator dried raisins will be lighter and slightly more chubby than those dried in the sun.

Note: Blend raisins into cookies, breads, hot and cold cereals, pancakes, muffins, puddings, stuffings, and salads. Plain, they make a terrific snack.

Nectarines 8 10 12 14 16 hrs

Although nectarines resemble smooth-skinned peaches, they have a unique taste all their own. Select nectarines that are attractively colored, plump, and have the slightest softening along the seam. A popular variety for drying is Mericrest.

Step-by-Step
1. Wash the nectarines and cut into 3/8" slices or circles.
2. Place on the dehydrator trays skin-side down. Dry until pliable.

Note: Experiment with dry and rehydrated nectarines in desserts like pies, cobblers, and cookies. They're equally good in breads, chutney, and granola.

Peaches  hrs

Next to apples, peaches are the most widely distributed fruit in the world. The two main types of peaches are freestone and clingstone, named according to how hard the pit is to remove. Freestone pits can be removed easily, while those of the clingstone must be scooped out. Both types of peaches are suitable for drying, but the clingstone usually has a somewhat better flavor. Select large, firm peaches with a white, yellow, or red flesh. Avoid immature peaches because they produce a poor dried product.

Step-by-Step
1. Wash the peaches thoroughly. If you wish to remove the skins, dip in boiling water for 1 minute, and then dip in cold. The skins should just slip off. Remove the pits and some of the surrounding red matter which can look somewhat unappetizing when dried.
2. Cut away the bruises and slice peaches into 1/4" to 3/8" circles or slices.
3. Dehydrate at 135°F until pliable.

Note: Peaches can be used dried or slightly rehydrated. Eat as a snack or in a compote with other fruits. Breads, puddings, upsidedown cakes, and cookies also benefit from the addition of peach morsels.

Pears

Giant Bartlett, Lincoln, and other late summer to early fall varieties are best for dehydrating. Winter pears, though not as tasty, will dehydrate nicely as well. Select golden yellow fruits with a rosy to red blush.

Step-by-Step
1. Wash pears and peel if desired.
2. Remove the stem and cut into 1/4" to 3/8" slices, or core and cut into quarters or eighths.
3. Dry at 135°F until pliable.

Note: Rehydrate dried pears and use like fresh or canned in cookies, cakes, fruit salads, and desserts. Dried slices taste great when stuffed with cheese or dip.

Pineapples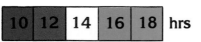

Pineapples should be a yellowish-brown color and fully ripe. Look for fresh, healthy leaves. A decayed bottom or dark, wet spots on the sides indicate overripeness.

Step-by-Step
1. Rinse the pineapple, cut off the leafy crown, and peel. (An electric knife will make the job easier.) Remove any fibrous areas that remain after peeling.
2. Remove the core and cut into 1/4" to 1/2" slices or wedges. If you are going to cut up more than two or three pineapples, wear gloves or occasionally rinse your hands in cold water; pineapples have a very high acid content.
3. Dehydrate the pineapple at 135°F until pliable.

Note: Dried pineapples, like persimmons, have a naturally high sugar content. They are unbeatable in granola, cookies, cakes, breads, puddings, and fritters.

Prune Plums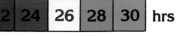

Plums particularly well-suited for dehydrating are called prune plums. Prune plums are higher in vitamins and minerals (particularly iron) than any other dried fruit. And since drying in an electric dehydrator takes only about one-fifth as long as old sun methods, more of this goodness is preserved. Leading varieties include California, French, Stanley, and Imperial. Ripe prune plums should be slightly soft and have sweet yellow to amber flesh. The thin skin may range from reddish-purple to purplish-black in color.

Step-by-Step
1. Wash prune plums thoroughly, cut them in half, and remove the pits. Pop the backs to expose more surface to the air and speed drying. To dry them whole, check for 2 minutes.
2. Dehydrate prune plums at 135°F until leathery. Whole prune plums may take up to twice as long to dehydrate.

Note: Dried prune plums are a tasty snack. They may also be rehydrated by steaming or stewing. Dessert soups, breads, strudels, garnishes, stuffing, and salads will all get a lift from the addition of prunes.

GOOD FOR DEHYDRATING _____

Currants

For another raisin variation, try dried currants. They're tart and tangy. Seedless black varieties make good snacks, while red varieties such as Red Lake and Wilder are fine for cooking. Both black and red currants grow wild in Western Europe and are easily cultivated here in America.

Step-by-Step
1. Wash and remove stems.
2. "Check" for 30 to 90 seconds in boiling water to reduce drying time.
3. Place the currants in the dehydrator at 135°F until leathery.

Note: Dehydrated currants are a good substitute for raisins in baked goods and hot cereals.

Papaya

Besides being a tasty fruit, papayas are also the source of the drug papain. Papain is an enzyme, similar to pepsin, that helps your body digest food. Because of this, it is frequently used to make meat tenderizers. Choose round, firm papayas that are yellow to dark orange in color.

Step-by-Step
1. Thoroughly wash the rind. Thinly peel, cut the papaya in half, and then remove the pea-sized black seeds.
2. Cut lengthwise into 1/4″ to 3/8″ slices.
3. Dry at 135°F until pliable with no moisture pockets.

Note: Eat dehydrated papayas as a snack alone or in combination with other tropical fruits. After drying the seeds, powder them to make your own meat tenderizer or grind them to make a seasoning like pepper.

Plums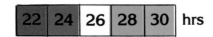

Plum pies and puddings are traditional Christmas treats, but you don't have to wait until the holidays to dry and enjoy plums. Popular plum varieties number well over 100, most of which are good for dehydrating. Pick fully ripe, sweet fruits that are undamaged.

Step-by-Step
1. Wash the plums and cut them in half. Remove the pits and cut into 1/4″ to 3/8″ slices.
2. Dehydrate plums at 135°F until pliable.

Note: Transform dried plums into plum pudding or add them to cookies, cakes, muffins, and breads.

Rhubarb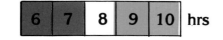

Rhubarb, nicknamed "the pieplant," is a unique vegetable eaten as a fruit; its initial flavor is sweet, but it has a tart aftertaste. Varieties such as Flare, Canada Red, Crimson Red, Victoria, and Valentine, with their vibrant red color and delightful flavors, dehydrate best. One caution: **Do not eat rhubarb leaves**; they contain poisonous oxalic acid salts.

Step-by-Step
1. Wash the rhubarb; then trim off and discard the leaves. Cut the stalks into 1″ lengths.
2. Dehydrate at 135°F until leathery.

Note: Cook dried rhubarb for sauce, add it to tarts and pies, or eat dry as a snack.

Strawberries

Gem, Streamliner, Superfection, Ogallala, and Dunlap are all excellent when dried. Pick large strawberries that are intensely red, firm and juicy.

Step-by-Step
1. Carefully wash, cut off the caps, and slice 1/4″ to 3/8″ thick.
2. Dry at 135°F until leathery and crisp.

Note: Dehydrated strawberries have a wide range of uses in pies, yogurt, puddings, frostings, fruit compotes, pancakes, and sauces as well as plain as a snack.

FAIR FOR DEHYDRATING

Blueberries

Wild or cultivated, blueberries are tasty when dried. The berries that you choose should be plump and fresh. They should also be a deep blue color such as Blueray, Rabbit Eye, Coville, or Berkeley.

Step-by-Step
1. Wash blueberries and remove the stems.
2. Leaving the berries whole, place in a colander and dip in boiling water for 15 to 30 seconds to "check" the skins.
3. Dry at 135°F until leathery and crisp.

Note: Dehydrated blueberries are a great confection all by themselves or incorporated into muffins, cakes, puddings, cobblers, waffles, pancakes, and sauces.

Kiwi

This subtropical fruit has a hairy, brown exterior and a sweet, green, seeded interior whose taste resembles a cross between a banana and a peach with a citrus tang.

Step-by-Step
1. Wash kiwi and peel.
2. Cut into 1/8″ to 1/4″ slices.
3. Dry at 135°F until leathery.

Note: Kiwi can be used as a garnish or as fruit compote, or it can be dried for decoration in a fruit medley.

Persimmons 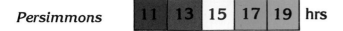 hrs

A persimmon is a small, yellowish fruit which is usually 1/2" to 2" in diameter. The sweetest persimmons are so soft and wrinkled that they almost look spoiled. Avoid unripe ones; they are extremely bitter.

Step-by-Step
1. Rinse the persimmons, remove the stem caps, and slice into 1/4" to 3/8" circles. Peeling is not necessary.
2. Dry at 135°F until leathery. Persimmons are done just as they start to turn translucent, but before they become brittle.

Note: Dehydrated persimmons are naturally sweet and can take the place of candy by themselves or in combination with other fruits. If they are dried until brittle, you can make persimmon sugar by finely chopping the fruit slices, and then pulverizing them in the blender. Rehydrated, they are delicious in puddings, cookies, and cakes.

POOR FOR DEHYDRATING

Certain fruits are more difficult to dehydrate with good results than others. This is not to say that you shouldn't try drying them; just don't be disappointed if your first-time results are unsatisfactory.

Avocados  hrs

Peel, remove the pit, and cut into 3/8" slices. Dehydrate at 135°F until brittle.

Berries  hrs

This category includes blackberries, boysenberries, cranberries, huckleberries, and raspberries. Wash the berries and leave whole or cut in half if desired for faster dehydrating. "Check" whole berries with a waxy coating for 30 to 90 seconds. Dry at 135°F until crisp and leathery. Cranberries should be shriveled and pliable.

Citrus Fruits  hrs

Slice the fruit into 1/8" to 1/4" slices and remove the seeds. Dry at 135°F until crisp. Use as a powder for flavoring in soups, fish, and salads or as a garnish.

Melons 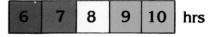 hrs

Slice watermelon into 1/4" circles or wedges; slice other melons into 1/2" slices. Remove any seeds. Dry at 135°F until watermelon is pliable and sticky and other melons are leathery.

FRUIT CORDIALS

Transform your dried fruit into fruit cordials. They're extremely easy to make, and their rich taste defies description. All you need are the following ingredients: 1 pound dried fruit (apples, apricots, peaches, pears, or prunes), 4/5 quart white chablis, 1 cup brandy, and 1 cup sugar.

Combine chablis, brandy, and sugar in a 2 quart glass or ceramic container that has a tight-fitting lid. Add the dried fruit, stir, and cover.

Let the cordial stand for 6 weeks at room temperature, checking it the first few days to make sure the sugar has dissolved. If the fruit is soft, remove it. The liquid cordial will be good for as long as you want to keep it.

CANDIED FRUIT

Candied fruit is very sweet; over half the fruit's moisture is replaced by sugar. The super-sweetened fruit is then dried into a candy-like confection. Use either fresh or already dehydrated fruit.

Preparation

Basically, you'll be preparing the fresh fruit in much the same way as you would for regular drying. After washing, prepare these popular candying fruits as follows:

Apples: Peel (if desired), core, and cut into 1/4" slices.

Apricots: Halve, remove pits, and cut into quarters.

Cherries: Remove stems and pit by halving or by using a cherry pitter.

Citrus Peel: Use only the outer 3/16" of the skin, avoiding the bitter white underlayer. Cover with water, boil for 15 minutes, and drain.

Peaches: To remove the skins, dip first in boiling water, then in cold. Halve, remove the pit, and cut into 1/2" slices.

Pears: Peel, core, and cut into 1/2" slices.

Pineapple: Peel, remove the thorny areas, core, and cut into 1/2" chunks.

Prunes: Halve, remove the stones, and pop the backs.

1. Fruit cordials require only a few simple ingredients.

2. Combine the chablis, brandy, and sugar in a jar. Add the dried fruit and stir.

3. In six weeks, the fruit cordial will be ready to enjoy. If the fruit becomes soft after a time, remove it.

Candying

Once all the fruit is prepared, you're ready to candy. You'll need a saucepan (large size), a candy thermometer, water, sugar, and corn syrup. (*Note:* The candying process will take a total of four days, excluding the drying time.)

To begin, combine 3 cups water, 3/4 cup white corn syrup, and 1 cup sugar in a large saucepan. Bring the mixture to a boil and add 2-1/4 pounds of fresh fruit or 6 to 9 cups of dehydrated fruit. Place the candy thermometer in the mixture and heat until it reaches 180°F. When it reaches that temperature, remove from the heat and let stand at room temperature for 18 to 24 hours.

On the second day, use a slotted spoon to transfer the fruit from the syrup to a dish; avoid transferring too much of the syrup. Add 1-7/8 cups sugar to the remaining syrup. Allow the mixture to boil and remove it from the heat. Spoon off any surface foam that appears. Add the fruit again and heat the mixture to 180°F. Remove the saucepan from the heat and let stand another 18 to 24 hours.

On the third day, repeat the procedure of the previous day, except this time add 3 cups sugar.

Finally, on the fourth day, again repeat the procedure of the second day, except add only 1-1/2 cups sugar.

Dehydrating

After the fruit has stood for the final time, transfer it from the syrup into a colander. To separate the pieces, rinse under cool running water; save the syrup for use as a topping. Arrange the fruit in a single layer on the drying trays and dry at 135°F until chewy. Candied fresh fruit will take only one-fourth as long to dry as its fresh counterpart. For example, fresh cherries normally dry in approximately 18 hours, but candied they will only take about 4-1/2 hours. After removing from the dehydrator, store carefully—candied fruit is extremely attractive to insects. High humidity may cause the candied fruit to remain tacky. If this occurs, place in the refrigerator till the tackiness disappears.

FRUIT LEATHERS

Leathers are dried, rolled sheets of plain or sweetened pureed fruits. (Vegetables or yogurt may also sometimes be used for leathers—see Chapters 5 and 8.) The produce is processed in a blender, spread in a thin layer over Teflex, kitchen parchment paper, or plastic wrap covered trays and dried to chewy perfection. Leathers are an excellent way to use drying leftovers or slightly overripe food.

1. To candy fruit, heat in sugar and syrup mixture, and allow to stand overnight. The next day, remove the fruit with a slotted spoon. Add more sugar and bring the mixture to a boil.

2. Remove pan from heat and skim off any resulting foam.

3. The finished candied fruit makes an attractive, tempting confection.

What to Use

Chop up nearly any fruit, vegetable, or combination of the two to make your leather. The produce can be raw or cooked, although the fresh flavor is often preferred. Choose foods that blend well together; mix up small samples and taste-test to see which ones you like best. Strawberry rhubarb leather and flavored yogurt rolls are big hits that cannot be purchased in stores. In general, any fresh, canned, or frozen produce is suitable.

Preparation

Wash, remove any bad spots, stem, pit, and peel fresh fruit if necessary. Drain canned fruits, and thoroughly thaw frozen ones. Cut the fruit into pieces, place in a blender, and puree until smooth. You may have to add a little water—keep it at a minimum—to firm fruits, such as apples, to start the blending process. For fresher flavor with canned fruit, add 1 tablespoon fresh lemon, lime, or orange juice per quart fruit. You may want to strain seedy berry purees before pouring them on the trays, but remember that seeds are an excellent concentrated food.

Some fruits like peaches and apricots oxidate rather rapidly. As an option, fruits can be heated to boiling prior to blending to retain their bright color. Other fruits can also be cooked if you want to alter the flavor of your leather, but cooking will decrease nutrients. Cool the fruit to lukewarm and strain or puree before pouring on the drying trays.

Sweeteners. The majority of fruit leathers are naturally sweet for the most part, but there are some tart ones like rhubarb and citrus fruits. In addition, many canned fruits are somewhat on the bland side. To perk up the taste, add honey or corn syrup to the puree. But don't overdo; use only 1 tablespoon per quart puree. Brown sugar also makes an interesting sweetening agent. However, avoid granulated sugar as it may recrystallize during storage and make the leather brittle.

Flavorings. As with sugar, use flavorings sparingly since they will concentrate upon drying. Add only 1/4 to 1/2 teaspoon of concentrated extracts or 1 tablespoon of fresh juices to the puree while blending. Try such flavorings as almond extract, lemon extract or juice, lime juice, orange extract or juice, or vanilla.

A pinch or so of spice or herbs is also nice. Find spices that mix well with the fruits and/or vegetables you are using. Allspice, cinnamon, chives, coriander, ginger, mace, mint, and nutmeg are all excellent choices.

Garnishes. Garnishes can be added to your leathers before or halfway through dehydrating and can include most nuts, coconut, granola, marshmallows, dates, and raisins. They give leathers that extra party touch. But don't reserve your garnished leathers just for company; they're too good not to be enjoyed all the time.

1. Preparation for making fruit leathers begins with washing, coring, and slicing the fruit. After these steps are completed, place it in the blender and puree.

2. Pour the puree onto the prepared trays, spreading it so the edges are thicker than the center.

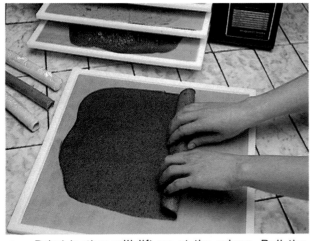

3. Dried leather will lift up at the edges. Roll the leather while it's still warm.

1. Garnish fruit leathers with any of a variety of toppings. After the puree has been poured out on the trays, sprinkle on the chosen topping. Leathers garnished with nuts or coconut should be refrigerated.

2. Small leather "kisses" can be made by dropping the puree on the trays in spoonfuls, garnishing, and folding over when dry.

Dehydrating

When the puree is ready, cover the dehydrator trays with Teflex, kitchen parchment paper, or plastic wrap; never use waxed paper, foil, or plastic bags. Pour on 3/4 to 1 cup puree per tray and allow it to spread out. The poured puree should be 1/8″ thick at the center and 1/4″ thick at the edges. The edges must be heavier; otherwise, they will dry too quickly and become brittle.

Set the thermostat for 135°F and place the trays in the dehydrator. If you rotate the trays 180° halfway through the cycle, drying time will be shortened. Drying time will vary according to the amount of moisture in the puree and its depth on the trays. For example, an apple leather may take 6 hours, while a grape one may require up to 10 hours drying time. However, 4 to 6 hours is about average. If you want to add garnishes during drying, do so while the puree is still moist.

When the puree is leathery and pliable with no sticky spots in the center, your leather is done. Peel up an inch or so of the sheet along the edge to check. If the leather meets the test, peel it off the Teflex, kitchen parchment paper, or plastic wrap while it is still warm; it should come off in one sheet with no puree adhering.

Storage

Lay the leather out on plastic wrap, roll leather and plastic up into a roll, and wrap thoroughly in more plastic wrap. This preserves freshness and keeps out moisture. (You can also cut the roll up into bite-size pieces and wrap that way.) Store the wrapped leathers in sealable plastic bags or airtight containers. Foil-lined potato chip containers and plastic buckets are good choices. Do not keep fruit and vegetable leathers in the same container; this could cause the vegetable leathers to mold. Store the bags or containers in a cool, dark place to prevent them from becoming sticky. Leathers with nuts, spices, or coconut included must be stored in the freezer or they will spoil after a month or so.

Using Your Leathers

You'll like leathers just as is, in lunches, or for snacks when fresh fruit is scarce. Or be fancy and fill them with caramel, chocolate, cheese, fruit, marshmallow cream, or peanut butter jelly-roll style. Eat whole or cut into swirly slices. (*Note:* Do not store leathers once they have been filled; use immediately.)

If some of the leather becomes brittle, don't throw it away. Instead, chop it up in a blender for leather chips. Reconstitute by soaking 1 cup chips in 1/2 cup boiling water for 10 to 15 minutes. Smooth in the blender and use on ice cream and yogurt, in milk shakes and cereals, or as a pie filling. Chips can be made into a beverage by adding 5 parts water and 1 part chips and pureeing.

1. Filled fruit leathers are a scrumptious treat. Unroll the leather and spread on the filling, keeping it away from the edges.

2. Re-roll the leather jelly-roll style. Avoid squeezing out the filling.

3. Cut the rolled, filled leather into slices.

Fruit Leathers			
Food	Combine With:	Spices, Flavorings, & Sweeteners	Garnishes
Apples	apricots, bananas, dates, peaches, pears, plums, raisins	apple cider, cherry juice, cinnamon, honey, lemon juice, mixed spices, nutmeg, orange juice, raspberry juice, strawberry juice, sugar, tangerine juice	almonds, coconut, walnuts
Apricots	apples, bananas, dates, pineapple, raspberries, strawberries	brandy, brown sugar, honey, lemon juice, nutmeg	almonds
Bananas	apples, apricots, blueberries, grapes, peanut butter, pineapple, raspberries, strawberries, lemon and orange rind	coriander, ginger, honey, lemon juice, mace, nutmeg, vanilla	coconut, pecans, walnuts
Berries	apples	cinnamon	
Blueberries	bananas	lemon juice	
Cherries	apples, bananas, black raspberries, pineapple, raspberries, rhubarb	almond extract, honey, lemon juice	almonds, coconut
Cranberries	applesauce, bananas, dates, oranges	honey, orange juice	
Grapefruit		honey	
Grapes	apples, bananas	honey, lemon juice	
Lemons	lime	honey	
Nectarines		honey, lemon juice	almonds
Oranges	bananas, pears, persimmons	cinnamon, honey, lemon juice, mace, nutmeg	coconut
Peaches	apples, pineapple, plums	cinnamon, coriander, honey, lemon juice, nutmeg	almonds
Pears	apples, bananas, oranges	cinnamon, lemon juice, nutmeg	coconut
Persimmons	oranges, pineapple		
Pineapples	apricots, bananas, strawberries	cinnamon, honey	coconut
Plums, Prunes	apples, apricots, dates, peaches, raisins	honey, lemon juice, orange juice	sesame seeds

Fruit Leathers (continued)			
Food	**Combine With:**	**Spices, Flavorings, & Sweeteners**	**Garnishes**
Pumpkin	apples	brown sugar, cinnamon, cloves, ginger, granulated sugar, honey, nutmeg	
Raspberries	apples, bananas, huckleberries, pineapple	corn syrup, honey	
Rhubarb	black raspberries, cherries, strawberries	honey	
Strawberries	apricots, bananas, rhubarb, pineapple	cinnamon, honey, lemon juice, mace, nutmeg	coconut
Watermelon	bananas, pineapple	lemon juice	

Note: To make a delightfully different leather, yogurt may be combined with many of the fruits listed in this table.

5

DEHYDRATING VEGETABLES

Vegetables—you could dry a different one each day for a month and still not go through the entire list. Some are more suitable for dehydrating than others but once you get started, you'll want to try them all.

What do we get from vegetables? Vegetables are rich sources of vitamins and minerals. Some of the important nutrients they contain include: vitamin A, vitamin C, niacin, phosphorus, calcium, and iron—all of which are preserved (although not in their entirety) when properly dehydrated. Peas and members of the bean family contribute protein. In addition, vegetables are vital suppliers of *bulk*, indigestible fiber that aids in the digestive process. One thing you probably won't gain from vegetables is weight. One-half cup of most vegetables contains less than 50 calories; starchy ones, like potatoes and beans, may have 50 to 100 calories per 1/2 cup serving.

To preserve most of this goodness in your dehydrated food, start with vegetables that are ripe and in prime condition. Buy or pick the crispest, freshest, most flavorful ones that can be obtained. Dehydrating retains most of the nutrition and good taste, but it can't improve on the original quality of the food. The fresher the vegetables are when processed, the better they will taste when rehydrated and cooked.

GENERAL RULES FOR DEHYDRATING VEGETABLES

Take extra care when drying vegetables because they spoil and deteriorate much more quickly than fruits. This doesn't imply that the novice dryer should shy away from them—not at all. Just pay close attention to dehydrating procedures given here and in Chapter 3, and you'll have great results.

Preparation and Pretreatment. Once you get the vegetables home, remember not to store them at room temperature if at all possible. If you can't dry the vegetables immediately, refrigerate them to avoid deterioration. Pre-

pare only as many vegetables as you can dehydrate in one load.

Wash vegetables quickly and thoroughly right before processing. Use cold, not hot, water to help preserve freshness and avoid careless handling that could damage the produce. Vegetables covered with dirt should be rinsed under cool running water and scrubbed if necessary. In any case, don't allow the vegetables to soak in the water. Soaking causes many water-soluble vitamins and minerals to dissolve and speeds deterioration.

Most vegetables cannot be dried "as is"; slicing or cutting is usually required. Peeling is a matter of individual preference, though certain vegetable peelings will toughen upon being dried. Remove any fibrous or woody portions, and cut away bruised, moldy, or decayed spots. One spoiled area may contain enough spoilage-organisms to contaminate an entire batch of vegetables.

With vegetables, drying time is crucial to tenderness. The longer the time, the less flavorful and the poorer the product. Drying time can be hastened by drying small, uniformly cut pieces. Thicker pieces result in longer times. For easier, quicker cutting, use a food slicer or processor rather than a knife when possible. You'll save your fingers from injury and the slices will be neater and more equal.

Vegetables such as green beans which normally require a longer cooking time may benefit from steam or water blanching (1 to 3 minutes) prior to drying. However, most other vegetables like greens or mushrooms need not be blanched before drying. Refer back to Chapter 3 for complete how-to directions for both blanching methods.

Dehydrating. Vegetables have a lower moisture content than fruits, so cooler drying temperatures must be employed. If the temperature is too high, the vegetable pieces will "case harden." (See page 23 for an explanation of case hardening.) Set the dehydrator's thermostat at 125°F and spread vegetables in a *single layer* on the drying trays. Leave space between pieces for better air circulation; do not overlap pieces. (*Note:* For tomatoes and onions, dry at 145°F instead of 125°F. In case of other exceptions, always refer to the individual listings before beginning to dry.) Different vegetables may be dried together as long as none are strong-smelling. Some strong-smelling vegetables include onions, peppers, and brussels sprouts.

Examine the produce from time to time until you are experienced enough to judge approximately how long each vegetable must dry. With a see-through door, you can look in without disturbing the drying process. Drying time varies with the type of vegetable, the thickness of the pieces, how ripe the vegetables are, the load on the trays, and particularly the outside humidity. A humid or rainy day extends normal drying time considerably. On an average, vegetables need anywhere from 4 to 14 hours to adequately dehydrate. But don't become upset if your time varies considerably from the ones listed; it can and does happen. If your model has a timer, use it. It will help you monitor the times without constant clock-watching. Also, keep in mind that rotating the trays 180° halfway through the process will hasten drying.

Testing. When they contain no more than 5% moisture, the vegetables are dry. Since there's no measuring device available to tell you when this point has been reached, you must rely on testing. Take a few samples from the center trays and allow them to cool. Feel and taste for the proper texture, which for most vegetables is somewhere between leathery and brittle. Again the more you dry, the easier it will become for you to judge these subtle differences.

When you're satisfied that the batch is done, turn off the dehydrator. The vegetables can be cooled in a bowl or right in the unit. Keep the door shut and you'll prevent dust from contaminating the food. In 30 minutes to 1 hour, transfer the food to the proper storage containers following the procedure given in Chapter 3. Leaving food in the dehydrator too long will cause it to reabsorb moisture from the air and become sticky.

Reconstituting. With the exception of certain vegetables like zucchini and potatoes which may be eaten dry as chips, most dried vegetables are used after being reconstituted and cooked. While you can kill two birds with one stone and rehydrate the vegetables as they are cooking, they will be more tender and flavorful if the rehydration is done as a separate step.

Place the vegetables in a container and pour on an equal amount of liquid. For example, rehydrate 1 cup of beets in 1 cup of water or beet juice. Cold liquid is fine, but boiling or heated liquid will shorten the rehydration time. (However, it will also begin to cook the food.) Soak vegetables anywhere from 10 minutes to 2 hours, depending on the thickness of the pieces and whether cool or boiling liquid is used. Soaking any longer than 2 hours could restart bacterial action, causing spoilage. Vegetables are considered rehydrated when they return to their near-fresh size.

Don't soak leafy vegetables like cabbage, chard, spinach, and lettuce; they are fine enough to rehydrate well during the cooking process.

1. The majority of vegetables, like green beans, require little preparation before pretreating. Slice beans into 1" pieces.

2. If you desire, steam blanch the green beans before dehydrating.

3. Dried beans will be shrunken and brittle.

1. Corn is one vegetable that should be pretreated for the best results. Leaving the corn on the cob, steam it until the milk has set.

2. Cut the kernels from the cob, and spread on the trays in a single layer.

VEGETABLE GUIDE

Here are most of the vegetables, from artichokes to zucchini, that you can dry in your dehydrator. Remember that your drying times may vary considerably from those listed here and that the pretreatment steps are optional. Use the humidity maps shown on pages 24 and 25 to approximate drying times. Match the color designating your area in the correct season with the square of the same color alongside each vegetable listing. The number of hours in the block will be your dehydrating time. For optional pretreatment methods, see the pretreating guide in Chapter 3.

EXCELLENT FOR DEHYDRATING

Onions

| 4 | 5 | 6 | 7 | 8 | hrs |

Onions are par excellent when dehydrated, particularly varieties such as White Bermuda, Red Creole, Downing Yellow Globe, Southport White Globe, Southport Red Globe, Sweet Spanish, and White Creole. Onions should be heavy for their size and have a pungent taste and aroma. Because of this odor, however, avoid drying them with other vegetables.

Step-by-Step
1. Remove the root and top, and peel off the paper shell.
2. Cut the onion into 1/4″ slices or 1/8″ rings or chop it. No pretreatment is required.
3. Dry at 145°F until leathery. Handle carefully as they readily reabsorb moisture.

Note: Dehydrated onions can be added to soups, salads, or cooked dishes. If you intend to convert them to powder or flakes, store as dried and only grate when needed for the best flavor retention.

To reconstitute, pour boiling water over the dried vegetables. Allow the vegetables to soak until they "plump."

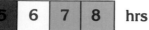

Beets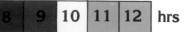

Select sweet, deep red beets that are about 2″ in diameter. They should have few to no side roots and should be a uniform color throughout. Varieties such as Ruby Queen, Detroit Dark Red, and Morse Red dry best.

Step-by-Step
1. Wash beets and trim so that 1/2″ of the top remains. Beets will bleed during cooking if the crown is cut.
2. Steam until tender, approximately 30 to 45 minutes.
3. Allow beets to cool, peel, and cut into 1/4″ round slices or 1/8″ cubes or shred.
4. Dehydrate beets at 125°F until leathery. (You may want to place beets on the bottom trays so they won't bleed on other vegetables.)

Note: Eat reconstituted beets as a vegetable flavored with sugar and butter, in soups such as borscht, or enjoy dry as a crisp snack with cheese dip.

Carrots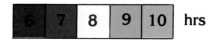

Carrots are rich and valuable sources of vitamin A, and contain substantial amounts of vitamin C, potassium, and natural sugar. Dehydrated carrots also have appreciable amounts of iron. Choose a variety such as Danvers Half-Long, Imperator, Tendersweet, or Royal Chatenay that has tapered, deep orange roots. Carrots for drying may be more mature than those intended to be served fresh.

Step-by-Step
1. Wash the carrots, trim tops, and peel or scrape if skins are dirty.
2. Cut into 1/8″ cubes or circles.
3. If desired, pretreat by blanching.
4. Dry at 125°F until leathery.

Note: Dehydrated carrots can be mixed in salads or gelatins. Dried shredded carrot is excellent in carrot cake.

Peppers, Hot/Chili

Chili peppers are anything but chilly. More chili peppers are produced and consumed than any other spice in the world. To dehydrate your own hot peppers, choose fully developed dry pods of dark varieties such as Anaheim, Jalapeno, Red Cayenne, Hungarian, Yellow, and Red Chili.

Step-by-Step
1. Wash peppers. They can then be diced or left whole. Peppers that are diced will have better color and aroma because the drying time will be shorter. When cutting peppers, wear rubber gloves to protect your hands.
2. Dehydrate chili peppers at 125°F until leathery.

Note: After dehydration, hot peppers may be ground to make paprika, cayenne pepper, or chili powder.

GOOD FOR DEHYDRATING

Beans, Green and Wax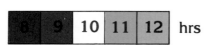

Snap beans were being cultivated in America at the time Columbus arrived and have long been a drying favorite. Strung up and left to air dry, they were known as "leather britches" because they resembled small, leathery pairs of pants. Unfortunately because of the long drying times, they often tasted like leather as well. Dried in your dehydrator, however, they're sure to rehydrate up tender and juicy.

Stringless varieties are best for drying, particularly long, plump pods that have a deep green (or yellow for wax) color and bright appearance. Look for crisp, fleshy walls and small seeds. Good drying beans include Roma, Tendergreen, Golden Wax, and Top Crop.

Step-by-Step
1. Wash beans and remove the pointed ends.
2. Cut into 1″ pieces or "French" style.
3. If desired, pretreat by blanching.
4. Arrange the beans on the trays and dehydrate at 125°F until brittle.

Note: Serve as a side dish cooked with pork or ham for added flavor, or combine with other vegetables in soups and salads.

Corn

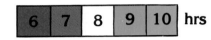

6 | 7 | 8 | 9 | 10 | hrs

Use only fresh, flavorful ears of such yellow varieties as Marcross, Golden Bantam, and Jubilee. Corn begins to lose its flavor soon after picking, so process immediately.

Step-by-Step

1. Shuck the corn, removing husk and silk; then trim the cobs.
2. Steam corn on the cob until the milk has set. Test by cutting a few kernels. If milk doesn't exude, the corn is ready to dry.
3. Carefully remove the kernels; try to avoid cutting into the cob.
4. Spread the corn on the trays in a single layer and dry at 125°F until brittle. Stir corn several times to facilitate drying.

Note: Dehydrated corn can be used for fritters, puddings, soups, stews, or breads, or it can be creamed as a side dish. Cornmeal can be made from dried corn in a grain mill as described on page 76.

Mushrooms

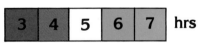

3 | 4 | 5 | 6 | 7 | hrs

There are over 38,000 known species of mushrooms, but only a very select few are edible. Beware of poisonous varieties! Dehydrate only safe species such as Agaricus and Boletus. They should be fresh and healthy looking with no signs of blackening. Small to medium sized mushrooms with closed caps will provide the most flavorful results.

Step-by-Step

1. Brush off any dirt and wipe with a damp cloth or quickly wash mushrooms in cold water; never soak.
2. Remove the woody portion of the stem and cut into 3/8" slices from the cap through the stem.
3. Dehydrate at 125°F until leathery.

Note: Rehydrate mushrooms and serve creamed, in omelets, in spaghetti sauce, or as a garnish. They also taste great in meat pastries and pies.

Okra

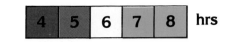

4 | 5 | 6 | 7 | 8 | hrs

Pods of okra for drying should be 2" to 4" long with a bright color; a withered appearance indicates unsuitability. To test pods for freshness, snap a few. The easier they snap, the fresher they are. Popular varieties include White Velvet and Clemson Spineless.

Step-by-Step

1. Wash the pods, trim off the stem ends, and slice into 1/4" pieces.
2. Dry at 125°F until leathery.

Note: Dehydrated okra can be used in stews, salads, and soups, or it can be breaded and french fried as a snack. Okra is also delicious baked in a tomato sauce flavored with salt, pepper, and onions.

Parsnips

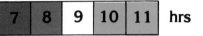

7 | 8 | 9 | 10 | 11 | hrs

Dry only fresh, tapered parsnip roots with white flesh and a hollow crown. If they are past their peak, they develop a disagreeable texture and flavor.

Step-by-Step

1. Scrub and trim the parsnips. (Peeling is optional.)
2. Cut into 3/8" slices or dice.
3. If desired, pretreat by blanching.
4. Dry at 125°F until very tough or brittle.

Note: Dehydrated parsnips can be baked, fried, stewed, or candied. They can also be eaten dry as a snack, plain, or with a dip.

Peas

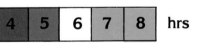

4 | 5 | 6 | 7 | 8 | hrs

Purchase young peas of a sweet variety like Little Marble, Perfection, or Thomas Laxton. If peas are too mature, they will be tough and mealy when rehydrated. Use only medium sized peas for best results. Crisp, tightly filled pods are a sign of quality.

Step-by-Step

1. Shell and wash peas within a few hours after picking if at all possible.
2. If desired, pretreat by blanching.
3. Dry at 125°F until brittle.

Note: Dehydrated peas are delicious in soup, in stews, or mixed with other vegetables as a side dish.

Peppers, Green or Red

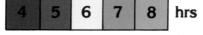

| 4 | 5 | 6 | 7 | 8 | hrs |

Select fresh well-formed peppers that have thick walls. Good drying peppers include: California Wonder, Merimack Wonder, Oakview Wonder, and Big Bertha.

Step-by-Step
1. Remove the stem, seeds, and white sections; then wash and dry the peppers.
2. Cut into 1/4" strips or rings, or chop in a blender.
3. Pretreat as described on page 21, if desired.
4. Dry at 125°F until leathery.

Note: Sliced, chopped, or grated as flavoring, dehydrated peppers are a welcome addition to any of a multitude of different dishes.

Popcorn

| 4 | 5 | 6 | 7 | 8 | hrs |

Although they didn't have movies, the Inca Indians of Peru were enjoying popcorn long before the first explorers arrived. Why popcorn pops always seems to be a mystery, but there's one thing we know for sure: It is definitely delicious eaten plain or topped with salt and creamy melted butter. The most popular species for dehydrating include White Cloud, Dynamite, and Japanese Hull-less.

Step-by-Step
1. Leave kernels on the cob until well dried; then remove.
2. Dry at 130°F until shriveled.
3. Make sure the kernels have been dehydrated sufficiently by popping a few of them. Popcorn must retain somewhat more moisture than other vegetables, approximately 10%, if it is to pop correctly.

Potatoes

| 6 | 8 | 10 | 12 | 14 | hrs |

Select crisp new potatoes that are mature and undamaged. The tubers should be smooth with shallow eyes. Russett Burbank, White Rose, and Norgold Russet are good drying varieties. Potatoes must be fresh to maintain their good taste when rehydrated; the skins on old potatoes will become tough and leathery. Preserve freshness by storing the potatoes in a cool place, but do not refrigerate.

Step-by-Step
1. Wash potatoes to remove dirt; peel if desired.
2. Cut french-fry style, in 1/4" slices, in 1/8" circles for chips, or grate.
3. Steam 4 to 6 minutes; then rinse in cool, clear water. Without proper pretreating, some potatoes may turn black during drying (see page 21 for pretreating instructions).
4. Dehydrate potatoes at 125°F. Slices and fries should be brittle to semi-transparent, and chips should be leathery. Test carefully since any lingering moisture can cause the entire batch to mold.

Note: Serve dried chips plain or with a dip. Rehydrate slices and fries and use as you would fresh potatoes in salads, casseroles, and side dishes.

Pumpkin

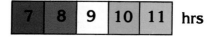

| 7 | 8 | 9 | 10 | 11 | hrs |

Carved as jack-o'-lanterns or plain, the pumpkin has always been the traditional symbol of fall and harvest time in America. But when dehydrated, you can enjoy pumpkin throughout the winter, spring, and summer as well. Pick pumpkins that have a bright orange color and a fine-grained, sweet flesh such as the Sweet Sugar and Spirit varieties.

Step-by-Step
1. Wash the pumpkin and cut into small pieces. Remove the stem, seeds, fibrous tissues, and outer skin.
2. Bake or steam the pumpkin until tender.
3. Scrape the pulp from the shell and puree in a blender. Two cups will make a 9" pie. (Measure before drying.) Do not add spices until you are ready to use the dried mixture or it will spoil.
4. Cover trays with Teflex, kitchen parchment paper, or plastic wrap and pour on puree.
5. Dry at 125°F until leathery.

Note: Dehydrated pumpkin puree is excellent for pie filling, as pudding, or in cookies or cake.

Rutabagas 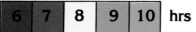 hrs

Rutabagas will taste somewhat like turnips when dried. The roots come in spherical and elongated varieties. Firm, sweet rutabagas with a light yellow flesh will taste best.

Step-by-Step
1. Scrub the rutabagas, cut off the tops and roots, and peel if desired.
2. Cut into 1/2″ slices or dice.
3. If desired, pretreat by blanching.
4. Dehydrate rutabagas at 125°F until brittle.

Note: Rehydrated rutabagas make a good potato substitute when mashed or boiled and are likewise tasty in stews. In the dried state, they can be eaten as a snack or in salads.

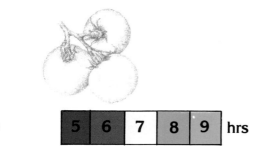

Tomatoes  hrs

This garden favorite was once thought to be poisonous because it is a member of the deadly nightshade family. Imagine—no spaghetti sauce, no ketchup, no tomato juice. Fortunately this myth was dispelled in the mid 19th century, and we now know that we can safely enjoy eating tomatoes. Although tomatoes are listed with and are commonly known as vegetables, they are actually members of the fruit category. High acid, full-flavored tomatoes like San Marzano and Royal Chico are best for drying; low acid ones will turn black when dehydrated. Use only dark red tomatoes with meaty walls.

Step-by-Step
1. Wash the tomatoes and remove the stems.
2. To remove skins, dip the tomatoes in boiling water, then immediately in cold water. The skins should just slip off.
3. Cut larger tomatoes in 1/4″ slices and halve the cherry variety. If you have an excess of low-acid tomatoes that you'd like to try to dry, puree them in a blender and add 1 tablespoon lemon juice or vinegar to each quart.
4. Dry at 145°F until leathery or brittle. (For puree, line trays with Teflex, kitchen parchment paper, or plastic wrap before pouring.)

Note: Chop dehydrated tomatoes for chili, soups, stews, and vegetable dishes. The dry puree can be powdered and converted into tomato sauce or tomato paste; this is a good way to make use of leather that has turned out too thin and brittle.

Turnips  hrs

Dry turnips that are uniformly globular with crisp, fine-grained flesh. The tops, which are dried separately, should be fresh and healthy looking. Popular species for drying include Purple Top White Globe, Golden Ball, and Milan.

Step-by-Step
1. Scrub well and peel. Remove tops and set aside to be used as greens.
2. Cut turnips into 3/8″ slices or dice them.
3. If desired, pretreat by blanching.
4. Dehydrate turnips at 125°F until very tough to brittle.

Note: Add turnip cubes to soups or salads, and eat dry slices like chips. Rehydrated turnips can be served as a vegetable like fresh turnips.

Artichokes 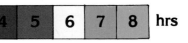 hrs

The Globe artichoke you will be dehydrating resembles a large, grayish-green thistle. Select healthy young artichokes that are firm and undamaged.

Step-by-Step
1. Rinse off and trim the leaves, allowing only the heart section to remain.
2. Remove any fuzzy portions and halve the heart.
3. If desired, pretreat by blanching.
4. Dehydrate artichokes at 125°F until brittle.

Note: Reconstitute artichokes in water to which lemon juice has been added to hold the color. They are best eaten when batter-dipped and fried.

Asparagus hrs

Asparagus is the "jet-setter" of the vegetable kingdom. Long an expensive culinary delicacy, gourmet restaurants around the world sing its praises. Join the "in" crowd, and dehydrate a good supply to have on hand for those special occasions. Popular varieties for dehydrating include Mary Washington and Waltham.

Step-by-Step
1. Wash the spears and cut off the tough, scaly ends. Asparagus does not store well, so begin processing soon after picking or purchasing it.
2. Slice the remainder of the spears into 1″ pieces.
3. If desired, pretreat by blanching.
4. Dry at 125°F until brittle.

Note: Serve rehydrated asparagus in a cream sauce, cheese sauce, or soup.

Beans, Lima 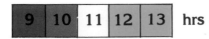 9 10 11 12 13 hrs

Because of their tough outer skins, lima beans dry rather slowly. So for the best results, make sure the beans you choose are fresh. Allow lima beans to become fully matured—beyond the table-use stage—before gathering. Pods should be plump with fat, creamy beans. Good varieties for dehydrating are Jackson Wonder and Thorogreen. The following instructions also apply to kidney, great northern, navy, and butter beans as well as to lentils and soybeans.

Step-by-Step
1. Shell and wash the beans.
2. If desired, pretreat by blanching.
3. Dehydrate limas at 125°F until hard and brittle. Beans should break clean when tapped with a hammer.

Note: Rehydrated limas can be used in soups or as a vegetable side dish served in a hollandaise or simple white cream sauce.

Broccoli  10 11 12 13 14 hrs

Like its relative the cauliflower, broccoli has thick flower clusters that form edible "heads." Choose fresh, healthy stalks with rich green heads and foliage. Buds should be tightly formed with a dark green or purple-green coloring. If the buds aren't tightly closed or the flowers have appeared, the broccoli is too old to dry. Top varieties for dehydrating include Italian Green Sprouting, Early Spartan, and Comet.

Step-by-Step
1. Trim broccoli and wash thoroughly.
2. Soak in salt water (1 teaspoon salt per quart water) for 10 minutes to remove hidden insects and eggs.
3. Rinse again to remove saltiness, and split lengthwise or in quarters.
4. If desired, pretreat by blanching.
5. Dry at 125°F until brittle.

Note: Reconstitute and add broccoli to quiches and soufflés or serve as a side dish in a cream or cheese sauce.

Cabbage  7 8 9 10 11 hrs

Market, Domestic, Golden Acre, Red Dutch, and Savoy are quality varieties to dry. White cabbage, used for sauerkraut, will not give you as good results. Pick only round, compact heads with crisp green to greenish-white leaves. Red cabbage should have smooth leaves with prominent veins; the leaves of the Savoy type will be wrinkled and blistered.

Step-by-Step
1. Wash the cabbage and remove the outer leaves.
2. Cut the head in half, core, and shred into 1/8" strips with a grater. The consistency of the cabbage should be a little thicker than that used for coleslaw.
3. Dehydrate cabbage at 125°F until brittle. Cabbage reabsorbs water very easily, so it must be thoroughly dry to keep well. Particularly check the spine section, as it will dry more slowly than the thinner leaves.

Note: Garnish rehydrated cabbage with a cheese, hollandaise, or sweet and sour sauce. It can also be flavored with ham and made into cabbage soup.

Eggplant 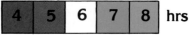 4 5 6 7 8 hrs

At one time eggplant was believed to be poisonous, but by 1860 these egg-shaped vegetables were being eaten with zeal. Choose ones that are young, tender, and glossy dark purple in color. Black Beauty and New York Purple are leading varieties for drying.

Step-by-Step
1. Wash, peel, and cut the eggplant into 1/4" slices.
2. Dry at 125°F until leathery.

Note: Substitute dehydrated eggplant for fresh when frying, in casseroles, or served in a cream or cheese sauce.

Kohlrabi  8 9 10 11 12 hrs

Developed from wild cabbage in northern Europe, kohlrabi had its debut in America at the start of the 18th century. Select white, green, or purple kohlrabi that has approximately a 3" diameter. The edible portion is the mild, nutty-flavored bulb which is also referred to as a cabbage-turnip. Purple and White Vienna are good varieties for dehydrating.

Step-by-Step
1. Rinse, trim root ends and stems, and remove leaves.
2. Thinly peel the bulbs, and slice into 1/4" pieces.
3. Dry at 125°F until tough and brittle.

Note: Substitute dehydrated kohlrabi for water chestnuts in oriental dishes and salads. It is also delicious creamed or cooked with butter and lemon juice.

Peas, Black-Eyed 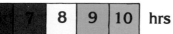 **hrs**

The black-eyed pea, or cowpea, grows wild in Asia, but it is cultivated in the United States. Allow peas to ripen completely and vine dry as much as possible before picking. Brown-crowder and purple-hull peas can be dried in the same manner as the black-eyed species.

Step-by-Step
1. Shell the peas.
2. Dry at 125°F until brittle. Dried black-eyed peas will split when tapped with a hammer. Time may vary considerably according to how dry the peas were when picked.

Note: Black-eyed peas are eaten as a side dish, flavored with onions and pork.

Squash, Summer 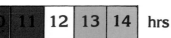 **hrs**

The word squash comes from the Indian word *Askutasquash,* or "eaten raw." Dry white or yellow varieties like Crookneck, Pattypan, and Early Straightneck. They should not only have a good shape and color, but also be young and meaty.

Step-by-Step
1. Wash squash and cut into 1/4" slices or into 1/8" slices for chips. Peeling is not necessary.
2. Dry at 125°F until leathery.

Note: Dehydrated thin squash slices can be nibbled on as chips or chopped and added to salads.

Sweet Potatoes (or Yams) **hrs**

Choose bright copper or brown-skinned sweet potatoes with deep orange flesh. Avoid using potatoes that are damaged or have wrinkled skin. Popular varieties for dehydrating include Porto Rican, Centennial, and All Gold.

Step-by-Step
1. Wash potatoes, peel, and cut into 1/4" slices.
2. If desired, pretreat by blanching.
3. Dehydrate yams at 125°F until brittle.

Note: Rehydrated, they can be used in place of fresh sweet potatoes. They can also be substituted for pumpkin in pie, pudding, and cake recipes.

Zucchini  **hrs**

Select slender immature vegetables that have not yet begun to form seeds. If you have older zucchini on hand, the seeds should be removed prior to drying. Older zucchini does not have a fresh taste but may be used for recipes requiring finely chopped or grated zucchini, such as breads and soups.

Step-by-Step
1. Wash, remove seeds (if necessary), and cut zucchini into 1/4" slices or into 1/8" slices for chips.
2. Dry at 125°F until brittle.

Note: Eat dehydrated zucchini slices as chips with cheese dip or chop and sprinkle on soups and casseroles.

POOR FOR DEHYDRATING

In the case of these vegetables, it's more accurate to say that they are poor when rehydrated—which is how dried vegetables are generally used. Leafy vegetables, on a whole, become limp and soggy when rehydrated, but they are very good when kept dry and crumbled as seasoning. In fact, you can achieve quite satisfactory results with the majority of the "poor" vegetables after just a little practice.

Brussels Sprouts **hrs**

Remove coarse outer leaves, and cut brussels sprouts in half. If desired, pretreat by blanching. Dry at 125°F, turning the halves over midway through the drying time. Dehydrated sprouts should be very dry and brittle.

Cauliflower 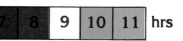 **hrs**

Wash the cauliflower, remove the flowerets, and cut them through the stem. Slices greater than 1" thick will not dry well. Soak in salt water to remove any insects. If desired, pretreat by blanching. Dehydrate cauliflower at 125°F until tough to brittle.

Celery **hrs**

Scrub the stalks and leaves to remove dirt; peel coarse strings and cut stalks into 1/4" strips. (The leaves should remain whole.) If desired, pretreat as described on page 22. Dry at 125°F until the stalks are leathery and the leaves are brittle.

Cucumber  **hrs**

Wash the cucumber and slice into 1/8" pieces. (Peeling is optional.) Dry at 125°F until leathery. Keep in mind that dried and powdered cucumber is excellent as a seasoning.

Greens

| 3 | 4 | 5 | 6 | 7 | hrs |

This category includes collard, mustard, watercress, and turnip greens. Wash greens and dry at 125°F. Dehydrated greens should be crisp and crumble easily.

Kale

| 3 | 4 | 5 | 6 | 7 | hrs |

Wash and trim the leaves from the stem. Dehydrate at 125°F. Kale is dry when it is very crisp.

Lettuce

| 6 | 7 | 8 | 9 | 10 | hrs |

Trim off the outer leaves and remove the hearts from the heads. Shred the remaining leaves or cut the head into quarters. Dry at 125°F. Dehydrated lettuce should be crisp and crumble in the palm of your hand.

Radishes

| 5 | 6 | 7 | 8 | 9 | hrs |

Wash the radishes and trim off the top and root ends. Cut into 1/8″ slices and dry at 125°F until crisp.

Spinach

| 3 | 4 | 5 | 6 | 7 | hrs |

Wash and trim the spinach leaves from the stem; cut larger ones in half. Dry at 125°F. Properly dehydrated spinach should be crisp and crumbly.

Squash, Winter

| 7 | 8 | 9 | 10 | 11 | hrs |

Wash the squash and cut it into pieces. Remove the stem and seeds, and bake or steam until tender. Scrape the pulp from the shell and puree it in a blender. Cover the drying trays with Teflex, kitchen parchment paper, or plastic wrap; pour on the puree; and dehydrate at 125°F until leathery.

Swiss Chard

| 3 | 4 | 5 | 6 | 7 | hrs |

Wash the leaves thoroughly. Dry at 125°F until brittle. The stalks may also be cubed and dried.

VEGETABLE LEATHERS

Vegetable leathers are handled in much the same way as fruit types. For pumpkin and squash, cook prior to pureeing. Measure the liquefied amount as a guide for reconstituting them for pies and puddings. Unless you are using low acid tomatoes, it's not necessary to cook them—just blend. If you are unsure about the acid content, add 1 tablespoon lemon juice or vinegar to the puree to prevent it from darkening. To make tomato leather for pizza sauce, cook the puree first to remove some of the moisture and then pour on covered trays to finish drying. Your tomato leather can be rolled right out onto the pizza dough, ready to sprinkle with zesty cheese and toppings.

Two of the most popular tomato leathers are sweet tomato leather and tomato-vegetable leather.

Sweet Tomato Leather. Small cherry tomatoes or varieties with high solid content are best for leathers. Wash thoroughly and remove stems and blemishes. Puree in a blender. Begin with a few wedges of tomato to obtain juice, then add more tomatoes to the desired amount. The addition of a lemon wedge and 1 tablespoon of honey per cup of puree makes a delightfully sweet leather. Dehydrate the leather until it can be easily peeled off the trays lined with Teflex, kitchen parchment paper, or plastic wrap and until the center is no longer tacky. Sweet tomato leather dries in 8 to 10 hours at 135°F.

Tomato-Vegetable Leather. Follow the same general instructions listed as for sweet tomato leather. Whirl prepared onion, green pepper, and garlic in blender until fine. Add diced unpeeled tomatoes, a few at a time, blending until smooth. (For a beginning, try one medium onion, one green pepper, and one garlic clove per 3 cups prepared tomatoes.) Add cloves or other seasonings as desired. Dry in same manner as sweet tomato leather.

This leather may be eaten as is or used with the addition of water and a little seasoning as an excellent tomato sauce. A little may be added to soups for flavoring. One-half to 1″ squares of leather may be used with dips.

VEGETABLE CHIPS

Dehydrated, thinly sliced vegetables or vegetable chips are a nutritious low-calorie snack. Try thin zucchini chips, tomato chips, squash chips, parsnip chips, turnip chips, cucumber chips, beet chips, or carrot chips with your favorite dip. Slice vegetables by hand or with a food processor and dehydrate as suggested in the Vegetable Guide.

VEGETABLE FLAKES AND POWDERS

Vegetable flakes can be made by crushing dehydrated vegetables or leathers in a blender, with a rolling pin, or between your hands. Use them to flavor soups, sauces, casseroles, and other dishes.

Powders are pulverized dried vegetables or leathers. A blender or mill will give you the finest texture. Onion, celery, and tomato are the most popular powders and make nutritious seasonings for soups, salads, and egg dishes. Mixed with liquid, vegetable powders make great baby food and juices.

Place thoroughly dry vegetables in the blender and chop until they are flaked. Use vegetable flakes as seasonings, in baby food, or on salads. Powders are made in the same manner as flakes, only chopped for a longer period. Vegetable powders are excellent for flavoring creamed soups and sauces.

Vegetable Powders		
Vegetable	**Procedure**	**Use in**
Asparagus	Place slices or spears in blender and blend until powdered.	Soups.
Beans, Green	Blend until powdered.	Soups and sauces.
Broccoli	Place broken pieces in blender. Blend until thoroughly powdered.	Soups and sauces.
Celery	Powder in blender.	Seasoning.
Cucumber	Blend until powdered.	Seasoning and dips.
Onions	Place completely dry slices or chopped onion in blender until finely powdered.	Seasoning.
Peas	Powder in blender.	Soups or broths.
Peppers	Blend slices until powdered.	Seasoning and soups.
Spinach	Puree in blender.	Soups and spinach pasta.
Tomatoes	Blend into a powder. Make sure tomatoes are completely dehydrated with no signs of moisture.	Tomato sauce, paste, catsup, juice, and soup.

6

DEHYDRATING MEATS AND FISH

The history of preserving meat by drying is as ancient as the history of civilization itself. Primitive man laid strips of meat out in the sun to keep it for wintertime use. Later, someone somewhere realized that smoked meat or fish did not spoil easily and had a distinctive flavor. The discovery that chemicals in the smoke inhibited bacterial activity did not come until many years later. Another milestone was reached when man discovered that by heavily salting meat and fish before drying, its flavor and storage life were improved. In fact up until the advent of refrigeration, most non-fresh meats were salted to an excessive extent. We still use chemical salt compounds such as nitrites today to preserve packaged meats and improve their color and flavor. (However, these meats have recently come under fire from government agencies such as the FDA for being potentially harmful to your health.)

Nowadays, "curing" is the term used to include smoking, seasoning, salting, drying, or any combination of these food preservation methods. That is, cured meat is meat that has in some way been treated to prevent spoilage. To preserve meat, it is essential that it be cured. Once used mainly by campers and outdoorsmen, today's dried meat now provides a handy, flavorful, protein-rich snack for the entire family. In addition, with the high cost of meats, more and more people are simply turning to drying as a way to get the most from their investment. While you must take care when drying meats, it is still one of the most effective ways to keep both raw and cooked varieties. There's no energy expense for short-term storage, plus you needn't subject yourself to the nitrites and other chemical preservatives found in store-bought dried meats. You can do a very satisfactory job of drying without them.

TYPES OF DEHYDRATED MEATS

The two basic types of dehydrated meats are: dehydrated cooked meat and jerky (meat and fish). With slight variations, the drying process is basically the same for both of them.

Most meats and fish are dehydrated in the same way as the fruits and vegetables we've already discussed; however, there are certain precautions you must take. As we know, meat is made up of both fat and lean portions; fish is generally classified as having a low or high fat/oil content. Lean meats and low-fat fish keep well when dried, but fatty ones will spoil quickly. Therefore, be sure to select only fresh, lean meat and low-fat fish for long-term storage. Remove any fat that is present. *Do not* attempt to dehydrate pork; use only lean portions of cured ham. You can dry some of the fattier fish, but they must be immediately refrigerated and used as soon as possible.

DEHYDRATING COOKED MEATS

Drying cooked meats is a great way to use up leftovers. It will also keep meat tender and suitable for use in sandwich spreads, stews, and casseroles. The meat you use should be lean and thoroughly cooked. When meat has been cooked in broth, it should be removed, drained, and chilled before dehydrating. Chilling causes the fat to gel so it can be easily removed. Trim any excess fat from the meat and cut it into 1/2" cubes.

Drying. When dehydrating cooked meats, work only in small batches with complete sanitation. Evenly spread the cubed meat on the trays. Set the dehydrator at 145°F. (Turning the temperature down to between 120°F and 130°F toward the end of the drying period will sometimes make your dried cooked meat more tender.) Make sure the unit runs continuously until the meat is dry, or spoilage could result. Most meats require at least 6 hours (some require as much as 12) to dry thoroughly and will be tough to hard when done. Remember the drying times given in this chapter are only approximations; your drying times may vary as described in Chapter 3.

Blot off any beads of oil that remain on the surface of the meat before storing. To use the dried meat, soak the cubes in broth or water for 30 to 60 minutes; then let them simmer an additional 10 to 20 minutes.

Beef and Venison

Making sure to avoid as much fat as possible, select a tender roasting cut and trim off any fat. Steam, braise, or simmer the meat in a small amount of water for about 2 hours or process in a pressure cooker for about 35 minutes. After removing the meat from the heat, drain and cover it to prevent a crust from forming. Chill overnight in the refrigerator.

To aid in dehydrating, cut the meat into 1/2" cubes of relatively uniform size. Spread the pieces sparingly over the dehydrator trays, and dry (approximately 6 hours) at 145°F. Stir the cubes periodically. Now reduce the heat to 130°F and dry till the cubes are hard. To determine if the meat is thoroughly dry, cool a cube and try to cut it through the middle. If no moisture remains in the center, then the cube will be difficult to cut. To use the dehydrated cooked beef or venison, pour 1 cup boiling water over 1 cup of the meat cubes and soak for 3 to 4 hours.

Ham

Be sure to use only lean, very well-cured ham. Trim off all the fat. Since the ham you buy in stores is already cooked, you can dehydrate it as is. However, further cooking at home will make it more tender.

Cut the ham into 1/4" squares or very thin slices and spread one layer deep on the dehydrator trays. Dry at 145°F for about 4 hours, then reduce the temperature to 130°F, and dry until hard and dried throughout. During drying, occasionally stir the pieces.

To use your dried ham, pour 1 cup boiling water over 1 cup of the ham cubes. Cover and cook over low heat for 1 hour. Use the ham in bean and cabbage soups, with green beans, or as a flavoring in meat dishes.

Poultry

Do not use duck or goose because the meat is too fatty and greasy, hence it won't keep well. Select only very fresh chicken or turkey. Steam or simmer the poultry till tender. Allow it to cool; then remove any skin or fat.

Cut the meat into 1/4" to 1/2" squares and spread in a thin layer over the dehydrator trays. Dry for 4 hours at 145°F and then at 130°F until the cubes are hard and dehydrated throughout.

To use dried poultry cubes, pour 1 cup boiling water over 1 cup cubes in a saucepan. Cook over low heat until tender (45 to 50 minutes).

Lamb

Select a lean roasting cut of young lamb, and trim off the fat. Steam until tender or process in a pressure cooker for 20 minutes at 15 pounds pressure. Let the lamb cool before cutting into 1/2" cubes.

Spread the cubes thinly over the dehydrator trays. Dry (approximately 4 to 6 hours) at 145°F, stirring occasionally. Then reduce the heat to 130°F and continue dehydrating until the cubes are hard and dried throughout.

To use dried lamb, pour 1 cup boiling water over 1 cup cubes in a saucepan and simmer until tender (45 to 50 minutes). One cup dried lamb cubes will yield 1-1/2 cups cooked meat.

JERKY

Spanish explorers were one of the first to discover this method of saving a bit of today's meat for tomorrow's meal. As these adventurers ventured through Central America and the southwestern United States, they observed Indians cutting meat into long strips and drying it in the air and sun. The native Americans called this strange dried meat "charqui" (pronounced "sharkey"), which was later anglicized into "jerky."

Making Jerky

Because it is only one-quarter the weight of raw meat, jerky has become a staple for today's outdoors people—backpackers, campers, skiers, hunters, and fishers. It's easy to pack, lightweight, and keeps without refrigeration. Of course, "armchair" sportsmen will enjoy its spicy taste and chewy texture too. Jerky can be made from nearly any fresh, frozen, or cooked meat, though beef and venison jerky are probably the most popular.

What will make your jerky special and uniquely yours is the type of cure you use. Many recipes are available, but it's fun to make up your own concoction. Jerky cures usually center around salt, but in addition you can use virtually any mix of the following ingredients: soy, Worcestershire, tomato, or barbecue sauce; garlic, onion, or curry powder; seasoned salt; or pepper.

Preparation. Pick a lean cut of raw meat as free from fat as possible; the higher the fat content, the shorter the storage life of the jerky. Or, make use of cooked leftovers, as in the case of poultry.

The best way to get uniform pieces is with a meat slicer, but a sharp knife will do the trick. If you intend to use a knife, partially freezing raw meat will make slicing easier. You can slice the meat either with or across the grain. Jerky cut with the grain will be chewy; cut across the grain, it will be more tender but more brittle. Cut meat into strips 1" wide, 3/16" to 1/4" thick, and as long as you want. Once sliced, cut off any residue fat.

Curing. To better preserve your jerky, apply either a dry or brine cure prior to dehydrating. *Dry cures* are salt and seasoning mixtures rubbed into the meat surfaces. *Brine cures*, or marinades, combine water with the salt and seasonings—hence the name "brine," which is a seafaring term for the salty sea. Meat is soaked in the brine till

1. To make jerky, begin by assembling the necessary ingredients. Slice the meat into 1/4″ strips using a sharp knife. Cut either with or across the grain, depending on the texture desired. If the meat is partially frozen, it will slice easier.

2. Layer the strips of meat in a shallow container. Combine all the marinade ingredients and blend well.

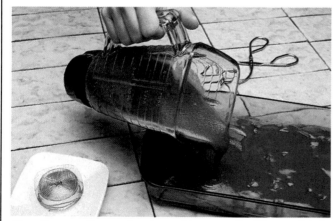

3. Pour on the marinade, making sure that it completely covers the strips. Marinate the meat in the refrigerator for 6 to 12 hours or overnight, drain, and dehydrate.

4. Package dried jerky in heat-sealed bags for best flavor retention.

the salt is absorbed. For both types of cure, any type of food-grade sodium chloride is suitable. Coarse pickling salt is often substituted for table salt, but never use rock salt as it may contain impurities.

The Process. To cure, spread the meat strips in a single layer on a cutting board or some other flat surface. For a dry cure, sprinkle the curing mixture on both sides of the strips. Make sure you coat the strips evenly. Layer the strips, one on top of another, in a glass, plastic, or stoneware container that is sealed tightly.

Meat for brine curing should be layered with the cure poured over it, covering the top layer. Place the container in the refrigerator and allow it to marinate for 6 to 12 hours (or preferably overnight). It is a good idea to turn the strips over several times to ensure thorough coating.

If you prefer your jerky smoked, it can be done before or after dehydrating. However, raw meat absorbs smoke more quickly. You can use liquid smoke, smoke salt, or mix a smoke flavoring right into the brine. A commercial smoker is another possibility, but the process is much more time-consuming.

Dehydrating. Shake off any excess cure and spread the meat strips in a single layer on the dehydrator trays. Dry at 145°F, occasionally blotting off any fat droplets that appear on the meat's surface.

Testing. The best thing to compare properly dried jerky with is a green stick. When bent, it should crack but not break. Always test using a cooled piece because warm ones will be somewhat more pliable. Jerky cut across the meat grain will be somewhat more brittle.

Various Types of Meat Jerky

Beef Jerky. Beef has been a food favorite since Biblical times. During the Middle Ages, the nobility regarded beef as one of the mainstays of their lavish banquets.

Flank, round, and sirloin tip cuts are the best to use when making beef jerky. Lower quality cuts are more fatty, giving you a higher percentage of unusable waste per pound—not to mention more time spent in trimming. Dry the beef at 145°F until pliable and leathery (approximately 4 to 8 hours). Your finished beef jerky will provide a nutritious snack for kids and grownups alike. Besides being rich in protein, beef is also high in phosphorus, iron, and riboflavin.

Ham Jerky. Cured ham is suitable for jerky; however, *pork should never be dehydrated under any circumstances.* The trichinella parasite and other harmful bacteria prevalent in pork are not destroyed by the dehydrating temperatures.

Start out with ham that is already pre-cooked and processed; this eliminates the need for any further curing. Dry at 145°F until the strips are hard and snap readily (approximately 5 to 5-1/2 hours).

Lamb Jerky. Since lamb is rather fatty, you must use extra caution when transforming it into jerky. The lamb you use should be fresh and processed immediately. Use choice leg or shoulder cuts for the best results. Dry at 145°F until pliable and leathery (approximately 8 to 12 hours).

Game Jerky. Deer, bear, and elk can all be made into jerkies, though venison makes some of the best jerky because it has no marbling fat. As with beef, your best bet is flank or round cuts. Before drying, game meat should be frozen for 60 days at 0°F. This should kill any disease-causing bacteria that may be present. To prepare, follow instructions for beef jerky.

Poultry Jerky. For something uniquely different, try cooked chicken or turkey jerky. It's a great way to use up Thanksgiving leftovers. For this kind of jerky, you can use the same cures as you would for meat. However since poultry is very fibrous, expect your jerky to be somewhat more brittle than its beef counterpart. Dry at 145°F until dehydrated throughout (about 4 hours).

Hamburger Jerky. One of the most unusual jerkies is made with hamburger. Start with very lean ground beef, or select a chuck roast and have it ground for you. Rather than curing, you will make the hamburger into a meat loaf-type mix by adding the following to the meat: (for 1 pound of beef) 1 teaspoon salt, 1 tablespoon Worcestershire sauce, and 1/4 teaspoon dried chopped onion.

Cover the trays with Teflex, kitchen parchment paper, or plastic wrap, and roll out the meat mixture into a 1/8″ layer. Dry for 4 to 6 hours at 145°F. Take out the trays, invert the jerky, and remove the tray covering. Blot off any surface grease, and then return the jerky to the dehydrator for another 4 to 6 hours until hard and leathery. Cut your hamburger jerky into strips before storing.

Pemmican. Besides jerky, the Indians made another dried meat product—pemmican. They used stones to pound the dried meat fine, and then combined it with fat, dried fruits, and vegetables. Start out with jerky that has been cut across the grain to make processing easier. Grind or pound the jerky into small pieces. Next, add an equal amount of ground or chopped raisins, dried apricots, dried berries, and dried peaches plus an equal amount of nuts such as peanuts or pecans. To this mixture, add a pinch of ground red pepper and enough peanut butter and honey to moisten the mixture. Blend well. Separate the pemmican into snack-size portions and package in plastic bags. Because of the fat in the nuts and peanut butter, pemmican will *not* keep as long as plain jerky.

Fish Jerky

Dehydrating fish is not a process to treat lightly. Even more so than meat, fish for jerky must be extremely fresh to prevent spoilage before it can be dried. Fish begin to deteriorate from the moment they leave the water; hot or humid weather only accelerates the process. For this reason, stick to working with freshly caught fish.

Another thing to be on the lookout for is the oil content of the fish. Fatty or oily fish, like tuna and bluefish, spoil rapidly and, unlike meat, there is no way to simply cut off the fat. For this reason, dehydrating these fish is unadvisable.

How to Tell if Fish is Fresh. Fresh fish should have bright, shiny, bulging eyes. The gills should be pink to red, clean, and have no disagreeable odor. Also check the scales; they should be glossy and fit tightly and smoothly against the body of the fish. Lastly, test the flesh; it should be firm and spring back when pressed lightly.

You can also use frozen fish. Store the frozen fish in the freezer compartment of your refrigerator until ready to dry it. Then, don't thaw the fish at room temperature; if you do, it will become flabby. Rather, let it defrost slowly in the refrigerator until it's supple enough to work with.

Cleaning and Filleting Fish. Cleaning fish is best left to neighborhood seafood shop owners. But if you're out in the field, the fish must be cleaned immediately and then preserved by cold storage. To clean fish for jerky, it must be skinned and filleted as follows:

1. Cut at a 45° angle through the backbone behind the head.

2. Slice down along both sides of the top, or dorsal, fin. Pull it out along with the bones. Do the same to the anal fin. Simple trimming with scissors will not remove the bones.

3. Using a knife or your fingers, pry loose the skin where the dorsal and head cuts meet.

4. Grasp these two flaps of skin and pull them down below the rib cage.

5. Grasping the meat in one hand and the head in the other, pull them apart.

6. Finish peeling off the skin.

7. Now you are ready to fillet the fish. Use a very sharp kitchen knife or a professional triangular filleting knife. A professional can do 27 fish or more an hour, but you will probably only be able to fillet 3 or 4 in that time to start.

8. Make a vertical cut running the knife along the ribs. Continue till the fillet is severed at the tail.

9. Turn the fish and remove the other fillet.

10. Wash the fish in fresh water, pat dry, and slice into 1/4″ to 3/8″ strips.

Curing. Make up a cold brine consisting of 3/4 cup salt to 1-1/2 quarts water and place the fish in it to marinate for about 1/2 hour. Rinse the fish thoroughly to remove traces of salt; then arrange the pieces on a cutting board. Coat the fish with a dry cure which may be made up of any combination of salt and seasonings. A typical dry cure recipe is given on page 127. Layer the coated fish in an air-tight glass or plastic container. To marinate, refrigerate for 6 to 10 hours. If the fish is steamed first, simply dry cure.

Drying. Remove the fish from the refrigerator and shake off any excess cure. Lay the strips on the dehydrator trays so none are touching, and dry for approximately 12 to 14 hours at 145°F. The dehydrator should be running constantly the entire time.

Testing. When you squeeze the fleshy part of a cooled piece of fish between your thumb and forefinger, it should leave no imprint. Properly dried fish jerky is firm and tough; it should never by crumbly or crunchy. Finish by smelling and tasting the fish. It should have a mild fishy flavor; regard any rancid odor as a warning sign and do not use the fish. Fish jerky should contain 15% to 20% moisture, but there should be no visible surface moisture on it.

Fish Guide

Some of the most popular fish you'll find in supermarkets and seafood shops are listed in the following column. Pay attention to those that are high in fat, and avoid them. (Some fattier fish, like tuna, may be incorporated in dehydrator-made crackers and other recipes.) Follow the general drying instructions covered earlier. Don't feel you've mastered the art when you've dried all those mentioned—there are over 30,000 varieties of fish in all.

DEHYDRATING SHRIMP

Dehydrated shrimp can be used in appetizers, soups, chowders, casseroles, salads, dips, and sandwich mixes as well as many main dishes. Either fresh or frozen shrimp can be dehydrated with equally good results. (*Note:* Frozen shrimp should be thawed before preparing. It can be quick-thawed by simply leaving it in the following boiling water solution for a longer amount of time or it could be covered and left to thaw at room temperature or in the refrigerator.)

To prepare either type of shrimp for dehydration, combine 2 quarts of water with 1/2 cup salt and heat to boiling. Add the shrimp, cover, and bring the water to a second

Fish/Shellfish	Percent Fat
Catfish	5.2
Cod	0.5
Croaker	2.5
Flounder	1.4
Greenland Turbot	3.5
Grouper	1.0
Haddock	0.5
Halibut	4.3
Lake Trout	11.1
Mackerel	9.9
Monkfish	1.5
Mullet	6.0
Ocean Perch	1.4
Pollock	1.3
Rainbow Trout	6.8
Rockfish	0.2
Salmon	9.3
Sea Bass	1.6
Sea Herring	2.8
Sea Trout	3.8
Shark	5.2
Shrimp	1.6
Smelt	2.0
Snapper	1.1
Sole	1.4
Tuna	5.1
Whitefish	7.2
Whiting	1.3
Yellow Perch	1.1

Note: Dry only low-fat fish, or those with under 5.0% fat. With fattier fish, the risk of spoilage is too great. (Table information by courtesy of National Fisheries Institute, Inc.)

boil. Reduce the heat and simmer for 1 to 3 minutes. The shrimp will turn pink when done. Remove it from the water, drain, and shell. If a sand vein is present, remove it by cutting lengthwise down the back of each shrimp and washing the vein out.

To dehydrate, leave the shrimp as is or cut into smaller pieces and arrange in a single layer on the dehydrator trays. Dry at 145°F until shrimp are hard and firm, approximately 4 to 6 hours.

To rehydrate the dried shrimp, place 1 cup dried shrimp in a bowl and pour on 1/2 cup boiling water. Refrigerate immediately. After approximately 1 hour, remove the shrimp from the water. Keep rehydrated shrimp in the refrigerator until ready to use.

7

DEHYDRATING HERBS AND NUTS

Using herbs and nuts, a little creativity, and some dehydrator know-how, you can add just the right flavor to virtually any food. Herbs and nuts are invaluable in the kitchen, and by dehydrating you'll always have a ready supply on hand. Both require little preparation to dehydrate; they're on the trays and done in the blink of an eye.

HERBS AND SPICES

As far back as the beginning of recorded history, people have been using herbs and spices as food, beverages, medicines, and in superstitious practices. Ancient Greeks and Romans ate parsley to keep from getting drunk. Hippocrates, "the father of medicine," used mustard in some of his preparations. In fact, if it weren't for the importance of herbs and spices to food preparation, we might not be living here today; remember that one reason Columbus was trying to find a shorter route to the East was to increase Europe's supply of spices.

What is an Herb?

Herbs are flowering plants that are valued for their flavor, aroma, and often medicinal properties. When you look at the entire spectrum of herbs available, you'll find that all different parts of the plants are used in cooking. For example, while basil, sassafras, and mint are grown mainly for their leaves, poppy, caraway, cumin, and anise are valued for their seeds. When it comes to dill, thyme, and parsley, both the stems and the leaves are used.

Many herbs and spices—such as mustard, parsley, and rosehips—are very rich in various vitamins and minerals. As with fruit, dehydrating intensifies their value, as well as flavor, by lessening the moisture content. This means you can achieve the same effects with lesser amounts—a savings no matter how small. Your dehydrated herbs will also be easier to store: 8 ounces of fresh herbs equal just 1 ounce after drying. Overall, drying is the easiest, most practical way to preserve and store these culinary aids.

General Rules for Dehydrating

Herbs and spices are delicate plants, and they must be treated delicately if they are to retain their valued aroma and flavor. Herbs should always be dried separately from other foods; the higher temperatures necessary for and increased humidity caused by moister food would adversely affect the herbs' quality.

Harvesting. Because the freshest herbs make the tastiest dried ones, you might consider growing some of your own. Select a sunny location for your herb garden, tend it regularly, and watch it grow. Many herbs—such as chives, ginger, mint, oregano, parsley, and sage—can also grow successfully indoors most of the year.

The actual time of year to harvest your herbs depends on the part of the plant to be used. Remove flowers when the buds are half open, but not fully in bloom. Harvest leaves when they are young and tender. Seeds are best when their color changes from green to brown or gray, but before the pods burst and scatter their contents. Dig out roots in the fall when the plant is fully grown.

When harvesting your herbs, always use scissors and cut them; don't pull or tear them out. If you live in a dusty or heavily traveled area, be sure to rinse off your plants the day before you plan to harvest. This will give them a chance to dry off overnight. Generally, the best time of the day to harvest any herb is as soon as the morning dew has evaporated.

Preparation. As mentioned, herbs and spices require rather simple preparation. First, trim off any dead or discolored plant parts. Wash off the leaves and stems of most herbs in cool water. A sink spray attachment is ideal for this purpose because it is gentle. Flower heads should be rinsed thoroughly before the petals are removed. Discard damaged parts. (Keep the heads whole for use in teas.) After it is sufficiently dried, remove the outer covering of the herb seeds by rubbing it between your hands. Be sure to dry the seeds thoroughly.

The possibility of insect contamination exists with some seeds, so it is a good idea to freeze the seeds for 48 hours prior to dehydrating. While not always necessary, the freezing method is still a good precaution to follow and will eliminate the frustration of drying a whole winter's stock of herbs only to lose it to insect infestation. However, do not freeze seeds that you intend to use for planting or they will not germinate.

Dehydrating. Your dehydrator will produce herbs and spices of the highest quality because of its controlled temperatures and air circulation; the old brown bag methods just can't compete. Preheat the dehydrator with the thermostat set for 95°F. Some plants may require temperatures up to 105°F, but temperatures any higher than this will ruin the flavor. Place the prepared plants on the trays in a sparse layer. When dehydrating large clusters, remove alternate trays so that the tops of the clusters are not touching the tray above. Most herbs and spices require 2 to 4 hours to dry completely, but some may take longer. Make sure you remove the herbs and spices from the dehydrator as soon as they are dry; dehydrating beyond this point destroys many of the oils, vitamins, and minerals. When tested, they should be crisp and crumbly.

Storage. Herbs, seeds, and spices have somewhat special packaging requirements. The containers must not only keep out air and moisture, but also light. Sunlight will fade the herbs' colors and flavoring oils. Dark colored glass jars are excellent for this purpose, but you can also cover clear ones with brown paper or black plastic. Never store herbs in cardboard boxes or paper bags; they are not adequate protection from insects, plus the paper tends to absorb the flavoring oils. Only keep what you will be immediately using in the kitchen; the moist air from cooking will cause the herbs to deteriorate faster. Smell your dried herbs before using. If the odor is faint or dusty, they won't be much good as seasoning.

HERB AND SPICE GUIDE

Included in the following list is just about any herb and spice you will ever consider using. These may or may not be familiar to you, so various flavoring uses have been included with each one. Most can be dried by following the general instructions given in the first section of this chapter, but step-by-step instructions have been included for special cases. Remember that most will dry in 2 to 4 hours, though this is *only an approximation*. When drying roots or such plants as comfrey, ginger, and horseradish allow more time to dehydrate.

1. Simple preparation is all that is needed for most herbs and spices. Discard any discolored plant parts and separate leaf clusters. Grate or slice plants such as horseradish.

2. Remove the herbs from the dehydrator as soon as they are thoroughly dry. Store whole.

Angelica

Angelica is a very useful herb because almost all of its parts can provide a delightful aroma or flavor to a variety of foods. Roots and tender stems can be candied and used in cookies and cakes. Stems can also be added to cooked vegetable dishes. Fresh leaves can flavor salads, fresh fruits, jams, and jellies. Even the dried seed may be added to cake and cookie dough. Besides its culinary uses, some parts of the plant are employed as medicines. The angelica plant can also be grown for beauty to give your garden a subtropical look.

Anise

Anise is a graceful plant with small white flowers and straw-colored seeds. Although its most well-known use is in flavoring licorice, anise also has ornamental and aesthetic value. Related to parsley and dill, anise is grown mainly for its seeds which have a spicy, licorice taste. They can be added to a wide variety of foods—pastries, cookies, candies, certain kinds of cheese, herb tea, salads, and spicy meats. The green leaves are used in salads, soups, stews, and for garnish. Oil extracted from the plant is a key ingredient in the making of absinthe, an alcoholic beverage. This oil is also used in perfumes and medicines, especially those for children's stomach troubles.

The large seed pods grow out of the flower centers. You can cut the green leaves as needed, but don't harvest the seeds until they begin to dry on the plant. If you pick them while they are still green, they will mold easily. The seeds are ripe and ready to harvest when their color changes from green to grayish brown.

Step-by-Step
1. Clip the seed clusters into a bag or basket to prevent them from scattering. The seed clusters should be cut approximately halfway down the plant. Cut the stems, and wash the seeds; if desired, they may then be frozen for 48 hours to remove any possibility of insect infestation.
2. Remove alternate trays in the dehydrator and spread the parts of the plant you wish to dry over the remaining trays. Dry at 95°F until the stalks and leaves are crisp.
3. Remove the seeds from the clusters and return them to the dehydrator until they are dried through.

Basil

This herb is an excellent seasoning commonly employed in Italian and Mediterranean style cooking. Its leaves add a pleasant, spicy flavor to tomato and potato dishes, vegetable juices, cheese and egg mixtures, salads, and many types of meat. Although it has a savory clove-like aroma, basil actually belongs to the mint family. The leaves must be dried quickly to avoid molding. Because of its very delicate nature, treat basil carefully to prevent damage.

Step-by-Step
1. Wash plant leaves the evening prior to harvesting; if the leaves are still wet, they may turn brown when dried.
2. Clip leaves before the flowers open. Subsequent cuttings may then be made.
3. Throw away dirty leaves.
4. Space the leaves on the trays so they are not touching. Dehydrate the leaves at no more than 95°F until the leaves are crisp enough to crumble in your hand.

Bay Leaf

A very versatile herb, bay or laurel leaves can be used to flavor soups, stews, sauces, meat, gravy, shellfish, salads, and cooked vegetables. Pluck and dry them any time of the year. Be careful to keep them whole when handling, because bay leaves are one of the few herbs that are not crumbled for use.

Step-by-Step
1. Pluck small, mature leaves from the stems.
2. Spread them over the trays and dehydrate at no more than 95°F until very brittle.
3. Cool and store whole.

Borage

Borage, with its sprays of brilliant bluish or purplish flowers, is grown in many apiaries because it is highly attractive to bees. Although it is used mainly as a garnish, the stems may be eaten as a vegetable and the flowers used to flavor lemonade or fruit punch. The stems and leaves may also be candied for use in cakes and cookies. Dehydrated leaves heighten the taste of cooked vegetables and salads, imparting a cucumber-like flavor. You can harvest the leaves when they are mature and pick the flowers after the first blossoming.

Caraway

Although this herb of the parsley family is best known for its spicy seeds, the leaves and roots are also sometimes used either fresh or cooked. The entire caraway should be dehydrated even if you plan to use only the seeds.

Dehydrated caraway seeds add extra flavor and crunch to sauces, soups, cakes, vegetables, and coleslaw. They can also be included in dishes such as pork and sauerkraut. Because caraway seeds are very potent, don't use an overabundance at once.

Celery

We've already mentioned celery as a vegetable, but it is actually an herb of the parsley family. The commercial production of celery in the United States started around Kalamazoo, Michigan sometime in the 1880s, but its rapid popularity soon spread its production to many more states. The stalk is often eaten as a vegetable, and the leaves can be eaten or used as a garnish. Generally, however, it is the dried seeds or leaves that are used as a seasoning.

Dried celery seeds can add flavor to sandwich spreads, salads, pickles, and relishes. While garden celery is the source of leaves used as seasoning, celery seeds are produced by a different type called "smallage." These seeds are very potent, so be frugal with their use.

Chervil

Sometimes called "cicely," chervil is an herb of the parsley family. It has fragrant leaves that smell much like anise. Sometimes used as an alternative to parsley, hence its nickname of "gourmet parsley," chervil is a frequent ingredient in French herb mixes. Add chervil to salads, egg or cheese dishes, cottage cheese, dips, sauces, soups, fish, and chicken. Because of its milder flavor, do not add until the dish is almost complete. Although chervil is generally dried only for its leaves, you can dry the seeds and use them for a seasoning as well.

Step-by-Step
1. Pick small bunches of chervil when the plants are mature.
2. Remove alternate trays from the dehydrator, and arrange whole bunches thinly over the remaining trays.
3. Dehydrate leaves at no more than 95°F, turning bunches once, until the leaves are brittle.
4. Allow the plants to cool, then store. Chop or crumble the leaves before using and discard the stems.

Chives

Closely related to the onion, chives are not only tasty, but also attractive as a garden plant or as a wintertime houseplant. Many travelers report seeing chives growing wild in Greece and Italy. Chives have an onion scent and a very mild onion flavor. Dried leaves enhance a variety of foods—salads, casseroles, omelets, sauces, cottage cheese, sour cream, vegetables, soups, stews, butter, and meat dishes. In addition, chives contain a fairly large amount of vitamin C.

Step-by-Step
1. Cut the leaves with scissors 1-1/2" to 2" from the roots any time throughout the growing season. Do not wash them, but discard any dirty leaves. Chop the remaining leaves into 1/4" pieces.
2. Spread the chives in a thin layer over the trays, and dehydrate them at no more than 95°F until brittle.

Comfrey

This little-known herb is loaded with food value, surpassing many common garden greens. Comfrey is rich in vitamins A and C, calcium, phosphorous, potassium, and trace elements. The leaves may also contain 20 to 30% protein. Comfrey is one of the hardiest vegetable plants you will encounter; it is virtually immune to garden pests. Pick comfrey in the morning after the dew has gone but before the sun is high, when its flavor and nutritional value are at their peaks. Dehydrated comfrey is valuable as a protein booster for broths, soups, stews, and casseroles. You can brew a superb tea by blending comfrey with mint.

Besides being a highly nutritional herb, comfrey is often recruited for medicinal purposes. It is used in poultices to alleviate pain, reduce swelling, and promote the healing of cuts and sores. Crushed comfrey leaves that have been wrapped in soft cotton cloth or gauze are applied to skin lesions in the treatment of such conditions as heat rash and poison ivy.

Step-by-Step
1. Pluck the developing center leaves near the crown of the plant. Discard any that are overdeveloped or soiled.
2. Spread the leaves in a thin layer over the trays and dry at 95°F until crisp and completely dehydrated.

Coriander

An herb of the parsley family, coriander has a very dominating fragrance that will overpower other seasonings if not used sparingly. Coriander is sometimes referred to as "cilantro." Actually, there is a slight difference in that coriander is the dried seeds of the plant and cilantro is the leaves. The dried seeds are used whole or crushed to flavor curries, sauces, liqueurs, candies, sausage, and potato salad. The leaves are added to soups and stews. Coriander is a popular seasoning in many ethnic dishes. Always dip coriander seeds in boiling water before drying to eliminate any insects.

Cumin

The aromatic, pungent flavor of cumin seeds is an ingredient in many spicy dishes throughout much of the world since Biblical times. A most popular seasoning for Indian and Paskistani cuisine, cumin seeds can be used whole or ground. Also try them in sausage, chili, game meat, and curry or fish dishes; use with restraint in cheese spreads and bread.

Step-by-Step
1. Allow cumin seeds to dry as much as possible on the plant, but pick the pods before they burst and scatter the seeds.
2. Spread the seeds over the dehydrator trays. If the mesh is too large and the seeds slip through, cover the trays with Teflex, kitchen parchment paper, or plastic wrap.
3. Dehydrate cumin at 105°F until the seeds are hard and completely dry.

Dill

Best known for its use in pickling and vinegars, dill is one of the most popular herbs around. Several medicines are made from dill, as well as various perfumes. A member of the parsley family, dill can also be added to vegetables, appetizers, most meat dishes, fish sauces, salads, coleslaw, sauerkraut, stews, and omelets.

The entire dill plant is valuable. The leaves can be used as a tasty garnish or to flavor soups, sauces, and stews. The seeds may be used in pickling and flavoring vinegar. They may also be used in coleslaw as a substitute for caraway seeds. Harvest before the buds open for the peak of freshness and flavor.

Step-by-Step
1. Cut the part of the plant you wish to dry, discarding the stems. Chop the flowers and/or leaves.
2. Spread the flowers, leaves, or seeds over the trays and dry at 105°F.

Fennel

Long a symbol of strength and valor to writers, fennel bears fine, threadlike leaves and many clusters of yellow flowers. It is grown not only for its strong licorice-flavored seeds, but also for its fragrant leaves. The seeds are used in breads, pastries, cheese, and confections. Try adding the leaves to vegetables, salads, stews, soup, seafood, or casseroles. Both seeds and leaves are used to flavor medicine and liqueurs. Some soaps and perfumes also contain oil of fennel.

Step-by-Step
1. Pick immature fennel leaves in the morning after the dew has evaporated. Do not wash dirty leaves; just throw them away. Harvest the seed after it has dried somewhat in the pod, but before the pods burst and scatter the seed.
2. Spread the leaves or seeds over the dehydrator trays; if the tray mesh is too large, cover the trays with Teflex, kitchen parchment paper, or plastic wrap.
3. Dehydrate the leaves at no more than 95°F; dry seeds at 105°F.

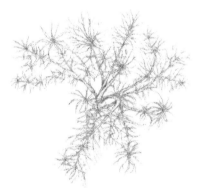

Garlic

Garlic, well-known for its strong aroma and flavor, is used in medicine in the form of a syrup and as a poultice for bronchitis. However, this relative of onions and chives is primarily grown for its pungently flavored bulb. It is said that if you dream of garlic, someone will soon discover your deepest secret. In folklore, garlic was widely reputed to ward off villainous vampires. Wreaths of garlic were hung around the supposed victim's neck and on windows to keep away the creatures of the night.

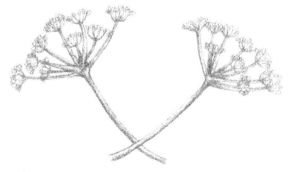

Used sparingly, garlic is one of the most versatile of all seasonings. It can be used to flavor almost any meat or egg dish, salads, salad dressing, vinegar, and breads. The garlic bulb grows under the ground with only the leafy top visible. When the tops begin to yellow and wilt, it is time to pull the plants.

Step-by-Step
1. Peel and finely chop the bulbs or cloves.
2. Spread the chopped garlic over the dehydrator trays. If the mesh is too large, cover the trays with Teflex, kitchen parchment paper, or plastic wrap.
3. Dry at 105°F until crisp.
4. Store dried garlic as is or as a powder; it can be powdered in a blender or with a mortar and pestle. Garlic salt can be made by briefly blending 1 part garlic powder with 4 parts salt.

Ginger

Ginger is not only a very popular food spice, but also an important ingredient in many other foods. It was considered to be an important item of commerce between Europe and the East during the Middle Ages. Besides adding flavor to foods such as candies, cookies, cakes, pumpkin pie, puddings, soups, meats, and vegetable dishes, ginger is also used in making many beverages— ginger ale, ginger beer, ginger wine, and ginger tea (a home remedy for stomachache). Oil of ginger is used as a medicine for stomach problems or for relieving toothache pain.

The spice comes from the roots. Fresh ginger root can easily be grown in your kitchen and is much more flavorful than the packaged ground ginger available in stores. To prepare ginger for dehydrating, grate or slice the root. As a powder, 1/8 teaspoon dried ginger is equivalent to 1 tablespoon grated fresh ginger.

Horehound

The common horehound is a bitter herb, the juice of which is extracted from the flowers and the leaves for making confections, cough syrup, and cough drops. Although it is not a recognized drug, horehound was formerly used for indigestion and as a stimulant. Dry the leaves to add a distinctive flavor to honey and herb tea.

Step-by-Step
1. Cut a few woody branches of the plant in mid-summer when the plant is covered with bud clusters. Cut or break the branches into 3″ or 4″ pieces.

2. Spread the pieces thinly over the trays, and dry at 100°F until dried through.
3. Store in glass jars.

Horseradish

The pungent flavor of horseradish is quite familiar to those who enjoy peppy seasonings. Horseradish is the bitter herb eaten at the Jewish Passover ceremony to symbolize the bitterness of their enslavement by the Egyptians. Belonging to the mustard family, horseradish adds zest to stews, some vegetables, seafood, many meat dishes, and white sauces. The hot flavor comes from the root, which is grated before adding to foods. Horseradish grows best after summer heat diminishes and the days begin to shorten; therefore, wait until after September to dig the roots. To avoid the strong scent of horseradish while drying, you may want to open the room windows.

Step-by-Step
1. Trim the tops and scour the horseradish roots with a stiff brush.
2. Grate coarsely or cut into 1/4″ thick slices.
3. Spread over trays and dry for 1 hour at 150°F, and then at 130°F until dry.
4. Use a blender to make horseradish powder. If you choose, the powder can later be mixed with water and used in sauces or dressings.

Hyssop

Both the leaf and the flower of the hyssop are used as seasonings. Dried flowers are used to flavor soups, stews, and herb tea. Dried leaves are used in vegetable juice, cranberry juice, and medicines. When added to bath water, dried hyssop leaves and flowers soothe and refresh the body. In the Middle Ages, sprigs were hung in houses to ward off demons and the dreaded plague.

Lemon Balm, Lemongrass, and Lemon Verbena

These three plants are all used to make a hot or cold, lemon-scented and flavored beverage or to add a tang to fruits, beverages, or herb tea. Cut long blades from the cactus-like lemongrass plant, wash, and drain well; use scissors to cut the blades into 1/2″ pieces. You will want to cut the leaves from lemon verbena. Verbena is also a good potpourri ingredient. Take sprigs of the lemon balm plant when blossoms begin to form, and chop the leaves and stems into 1″ pieces. Lemon balm is also known as the "honey plant" because it attracts bees. The dried leaves can be crushed in a muslin bag and added to bath water or steeped in white wine to revive the spirit.

Step-by-Step
1. Spread the plant parts thinly over the dehydrator trays.
2. Dry at 95°F until crisp enough to crumble in your hands.
3. Allow the dried plants to cool; then store in glass jars away from heat and light. Crumble to use.

Lovage

Lovage is grown for use as a garnish and for its aromatic seeds which are used for flavoring confections. The leaves, seeds, and roots of this celery-flavored plant are dried to flavor soups, stews, sauces, and casseroles.

Marjoram

A variety of the mint family, marjoram is one of the more useful herbs. Although it is slightly milder and sweeter than oregano, the two spices can sometimes be used interchangeably. Use marjoram sparingly until you are accustomed to its spicy flavor. The leaves are used as a garnish or dried and crumbled as a seasoning for many meat and egg dishes, stuffing, salads, stews, gravies, and various vegetables. Marjoram is especially popular in Italian dishes. The stems and flowers can also be dried and used as seasoning. Manufacturers use the oil from the plant in making soaps.

Step-by-Step
1. Pick the gray-green leaves when they are mature. Do not pretreat and do not wash. Discard any soiled leaves.
2. Spread leaves thinly over the trays and dry at 95°F until crisp enough to crumble in your hands.

Mint

Mint is the name of a whole family of plants which have a similar structure and a sometimes distinctive aroma and flavor. Certain kinds of mint are valuable in cooking, medicine, and perfume making. About 3,200 different kinds of mint grow throughout the world, but the best known members of the mint family are: basil, catnip, horehound, hyssop, marjoram, pennyroyal, peppermint, rosemary, sage, spearmint, and thyme. The leaf is the most flavorful part of the plant. If leaves are dried quickly and carefully, you can preserve much of the mint flavor for use throughout the year. Dried mint leaves add a delightful flavor to jellies, some meats, cooked vegetables, lemonade and other cool drinks, tea, candies, and baked goods.

Step-by-Step
1. The best time to pick mint leaves is in the early summer when the leaves are the most fragrant. However, you can pick them throughout the growing season if you wish.
2. Spread the leaves thinly over the trays and dry at no more than 95°F until crisp.
3. Crush the leaves just before adding to food.

Mustard

Mustard is the name of a family of plants which are grown for their abundant leaves and spicy seeds. In addition, mustard greens are an excellent source of calcium; iron; phosphorus; and vitamins A, B, and C; and their bulk and fiber have a mild laxative effect.

Dried mustard seeds are used in pickling, salad dressing, sauerkraut, corned beef, cooked cabbage, and various meat dishes. An oil within the mustard seed gives it its high flavor and also makes it a valuable household remedy. It can be used in a plaster to relieve pain. The two most common types of mustard seeds are the tangy dark brown seeds and the mild yellow ones.

Onion

Often categorized as a vegetable, onion is also a popular seasoning. Sliced, chopped, or powdered onion is added to all types of meat dishes, salads, vegetables, soups, casseroles, and much more. Storage is crucial if dried onions are to have a long shelf life. Leave slices whole until ready to use. No pretreatment is needed before drying. (For drying instructions, see Chapter 5.)

Oregano

Oregano is grown for both its flowers and its leaves. It is a strong-tasting herb (much stronger than its close relative marjoram). The name oregano is Spanish, and this herb was probably used by people of the Mediterranean area long before the Christian era. It makes a zesty addition to tomato dishes such as spaghetti sauce, pizza, cavatini, and lasagna. Oregano is popular in Italian, Greek, and Mexican foods; pork roast; beef stew; omelets; and especially wild game. Because of its potent flavor, use oregano sparingly at first. For the tastiest oregano, dry as quickly as possible.

Step-by-Step

1. Pick the flowers and outer leaves just as the flower begins to open.
2. Spread in a thin layer over the trays and dry at no more than 95°F until crisp.
3. Crumble in your hands before using.

Parsley

Parsley not only has an appealing appearance and pleasant taste, but it also has a higher food value than most herbs and is often considered to be a vegetable. It is an excellent source of vitamins A and C and many minerals, especially iron. Chewing on a sprig of fresh parsley can help to counter the effects of garlic and other strong spices on the breath. The most flavorful dried parsleys are Italian, Evergeen, and Moss-Curled. Seal your dehydrated parsley very tightly, as it has a tendency to reabsorb moisture from the air.

Step-by-Step

1. Wash the parsley lightly under cold running water. Separate clusters and throw away the long or tough stems.
2. Spread the sprigs or chopped leaves over the dehydrator trays.
3. Dry for approximately 1 hour at no more than 95°F until crisp and papery.
4. Store in small airtight containers, and crush before using.

Pennyroyal

A pleasant mint-flavored herb, pennyroyal adds a delightful touch to herbal teas. The American pennyroyal is an erect, slender plant commonly found in fields and along roadsides in the East. The leaves are sometimes used in household medicine.

Pepper

Pepper refers to a family of plants popular for their spicy berries. The sharp, biting taste is chiefly due to an acrid resin and oil. Pepper also has medicinal value and has been known to be used as a deterrent for ants. Be prudent when using hot varieties until you are accustomed to them.

Step-by-Step

1. Spread the whole, cut, or sliced peppers over the dehydrator trays.
2. Dry at 95°F until hard and brittle, stirring once or twice.

Rose

"That which we call a rose by any other name would smell as sweet." Shakespeare had his star-crossed heroine, Juliet, utter this line in one of the most important scenes in *Romeo and Juliet*. Since ancient times, the rose has been grown for its beautiful fragrant flowers, its attractive foliage, and its handsome fruits called hips. Dried rose petals can be used to flavor jams and jellies, baked fruits, and herb tea. Rose hips can also be used in tea. Although the hips have little flavor, they are a rich winter source of vitamin C—particularly those from the wild rose. Rose hip tea benefits from the addition of other herbs such as lemon balm and mint.

Step-by-Step

1. If you are growing your own rose bushes, cut the partially dried rose hips in the late fall after the leaves have dropped.
2. Spread slices thinly over the dehydrator trays.
3. Stirring occasionally, dry hips at 95°F until crisp and hard.

Rosemary

The oil from rosemary is used in perfume making, and its leaves impart a special flavor to sauces, soups, egg dishes, salad dressings, and many vegetables. Rosemary keeps most of its sweet flavor when dried. Do not cook dried rosemary, but soak it a few minutes in liquid to revive its flavor.

Step-by-Step

1. Do not wash the leaves, but discard those that are soiled.

2. Spread the leaves in a thin layer over the dehydrator trays.
3. Dry at no more than 95°F until crisp.
4. Finely crush with a rolling pin before using.

Sage

This hardy shrub is native to the Mediterranean region and has long been cultivated in gardens as a culinary and medicinal plant. In the months of June and July, it blooms a bright crimson-red. Another member of the mint family, sage is used mainly in poultry dishes. Its leaves can also add flavor to other meat dishes, dressings, gravies, cheeses, and omelets.

Step-by-Step
1. Discard the soiled leaves; do not wash.
2. Spread the leaves thinly over the dehydrator trays.
3. Dry at no more than 95°F.
4. Before using, crumble the leaves coarsely in your hands to release the full flavor. Discard any stems.

Sassafras

A handsome tree of the laurel family, sassafras is pyramidal in form and may reach heights of 60' to 90'. Almost any portion of the sassafras tree may be dried and used to make a delicious herb tea—once considered to be a spring "tonic." Dried leaves are also used in soups and vegetable dishes. A fine powder of dried sassafras leaves is often called filé powder, a popular ingredient in Creole dishes.

Step-by-Step
1. Pick young tender leaves in the spring. Harvest the bark or root in the early fall; cut into shavings, chop fine, or grind.
2. Spread thinly over the dehydrator trays.
3. Dry the leaves at no more than 95°F until crisp; dry the bark or root at 100°F.
4. Cool and store.

Savory

Two basic varieties of savory are available: summer and winter savory. Although they differ in color and size, the flavor is quite similar. Both savories are supposed to give quick relief from a bee sting. Often used as a garnish, fresh savory smells like grass and has a mild peppery flavor. Do not wash the leaves, but discard any soiled ones. Dried leaves are used to season dressings, salads, stews, vegetable juices, game, and poultry.

Sorrel

Also called sheep sorrel or sour dock, sorrel is a small herb of the buckwheat family. Its creeping habit makes it a troublesome weed in lawns. Dried sorrel leaves add flavor to soups, stews, omelets, cooked vegetables, and casseroles.

Tansy

Tansy is often grown in gardens for its insect-repelling properties. Dried tansy leaves are crushed and added to omelets and fish and meat dishes, or they can be brewed into herb tea. Tansy was once widely used for medicinal purposes and is still sometimes used as a household remedy for rheumatism and bruises.

Tarragon

The slightly sweet flavor of tarragon leaves is used to season many types of meats, tomato dishes, seafood, eggs, pickles, cookies, and vinegar. The leaves are also used to make cooking oil. Dehydrated tarragon loses its flavor quickly; therefore, take extra precautions when packaging.

Thyme

Thyme is a fragrant herb belonging to the mint family. The aromatic oil in the leaves and stem is used to make the drug thymol and to perfume toiletries. Thyme, one of the most familiar herbs, has a relatively mild flavor that faintly resembles that of oregano. Use sparingly until you become accustomed to its taste. Try adding thyme to meat dishes, soups, salads, dressings, gravies, and omelets. It is also good in most Italian dishes, macaroni and cheese, and tuna-noodle casserole.

Step-by-Step
1. Pick leaves when the plants first begin to flower. Discard any soiled leaves, but do not wash.
2. Spread the leaves in a thin layer over the dehydrator trays.
3. Dry at 95°F until crisp.
4. Crumble before using.

Woodruff

Also known as sweet woodruff, this herb is often grown as a border or rock garden plant. The woodruff plant has spiral leaves and clusters of funnel-shaped flowers. The dried leaves are used in wines, herb tea, and sachets.

HERB TEAS

Many of the common herbs described in this chapter can be used to make deliciously fragrant herb tea. You may wish to try any of the following alone or in combination: anise, borage, comfrey, dill, fennel, horehound, hyssop, lemon balm, lemongrass, lemon verbena, lovage, mint, pennyroyal, sage, sassafras, tansy, and woodruff. Other tantalizing additions to herb teas include cinnamon, cloves, fruit slices, nutmeg, ginger, raisins, wild cherries, or a slice of rose hip. The possibilities are limited only by your imagination and taste.

When mixing an herb tea, combine the dry ingredients, then label and store in glass jars. This method allows you to mix your favorite cup of tea at any time. Herb teas are also delicious iced when the summer sun parches your throat. Try these recipes for starters:

Fennel Clove Delight

Mix 4 ounces whole dried fennel seed with 2 ounces whole cloves and 1 ounce ground cloves. To make a cup, pour boiling water over 1 tablespoon of the crushed mixture. Cover and steep 3 to 5 minutes; then strain. This tea needs no sweetener.

Raspberry Star

Crush 2 ounces of star anise seeds with 4 ounces of dried raspberry leaves. To make a cup, use 1 tablespoon of the tea mix and steep in boiling water 5 to 7 minutes. Strain and garnish with a whole star anise.

Cinna-Mint

Blend 4 ounces dried mint leaves with 6 well-crushed cinnamon sticks and 2 tablespoons ground cinnamon. To make a cup, use 1 tablespoon of the tea and steep in boiling water for 3 minutes, then strain. If desired, add honey, a fresh cinnamon stick, or a sprig of fresh mint.

Citrus Spice

Mix 4 ounces of either lemon verbena leaves or lemon balm leaves, 2 ounces whole clove buds, 2 ounces candied orange peel, and 1 tablespoon grated, dried ginger root. To make a cup, put 1 tablespoon of the slightly crushed mixture in 1 cup boiling water. Cover and steep for 5 minutes. Strain and garnish with lemon, lime, or orange.

Ginger Zip

Mix 1 ounce grated ginger root, 1 ounce fennel seed, 1/2 of a grated nutmeg, and 2 tablespoons dried lemon peel. To make a cup, place 1 teaspoon of the mixture in 1 cup boiling water and steep for 5 minutes. Strain, and dilute to taste.

GOURMET HERB SEASONINGS

Convert your dried herbs into flavorful home-blended vinegars, herb salts, and seasoning mixes. They're great for gifts and offer convenience to good cooks without sacrificing culinary appeal.

To make herb vinegars, first gather an assortment of corked or lidded bottles and cruets. Next choose red, white, or malt vinegar as a base, keeping in mind the herbs you plan to use. Traditional wine vinegars include basil, tarragon, and garlic, but any favorite herb will make a zesty vinegar. An Italian mixture for salads might include oregano, basil, garlic, and thyme. A fish-and-chips favorite combines dill in malt vinegar. Rosemary in red wine vinegar is a perfect complement to robust red meat and lamb dishes.

To make any herb vinegar, add 2 ounces of dried herb to each quart of vinegar. Bring the herbs and vinegar to a boil, simmer 15 minutes, strain, and pour into clean bottles. If you like, place a sprig of herb in the bottled vinegar for decoration and added flavor. A hot wax seal with a pinch of allspice or cinnamon added is an elegant touch. Label each herb vinegar and store in a dark, cool place until ready to use.

Your own herb vinegar will make any salad special. (See page 97 for recipe.)

Gourmet salts require only uniodized salt, your dried herbs, and a little bit of your time. Place salt in a heavy glass bowl and sprinkle with dried herbs. Remember that dried herbs are more concentrated, so use only about half as much as you would fresh. Thoroughly crush and blend the mixture with a wooden spoon. (You could also use a mortar and pestle.) Add a pinch of pepper or paprika for variety. Pack into small lidded bottles and label for future use.

Lemon pepper is a spicy complement to any herb salt.

Mix 1 tablespoon dried lemon peel with 6 teaspoons coarse black pepper, 2 tablespoons coarse salt, and 1 tablespoon dried minced garlic. When well blended, the lemon pepper can be poured into a jar that matches the herb salt jar. In a gift box, a jar each of lemon pepper and herb salt are a dynamic duo.

Herb seasoning mixes are another gourmet delight. Make a salad dressing blend of dried celery leaves, basil, and thyme; or make a soup blend of dried bay leaf, oregano, rosemary, and sage. Mix up a batch of bouquet garnish herbs for fish, stews, and stockpots by combining 1 crumbled bay leaf, 1 tablespoon dried parsley, 1 tablespoon dried tarragon, and 1 teaspoon each of dried thyme and rosemary. French "fines herbes" is a delicate mingling of dried parsley, chervil, chives, and tarragon in equal proportions.

Package herb seasonings in small jars for use by the teaspoonful, or sew up tiny string-tied muslin bags with a teaspoon of herbs in each. The little bags can be dropped right into boiling stock, removed when cooking is done, frozen, and reused once more before either being refilled with fresh mix or discarded.

Herbal Skin Astringent

Herbal mixtures help restore the skin's natural pH balance. The following mixture is excellent for an overall face and body astringent as well as a super cleansing hair rinse:

Combine 1/4 cup of each:
> dried orange peel
> dried orange leaves
> dried orange flowers
> dried rose leaves
> dried rose buds (and petals)
> dried rose hips
> dried camomile
> dried white willow bark (may be obtained from health food store)

1. To the above mixture, add 1 quart boiling vinegar.
2. Steep in a glass container, shaking daily for approximately 3 to 5 days or until the herbs have lost their color.
3. Strain. Add 1 cup rose water and let mixture settle for approximately 1 week.
4. Move clear mixture to a clean glass container, discarding sediment.

NUTS

Nuts are the dry one-seeded fruits of any of a number of shrubs and trees. The term "nut" may refer to the woody shell (or *husk*) and the edible inner *kernel*, or it may refer just to the kernel alone. Nuts provide a concentrated source of protein, and many are rich in fats as well. Some of the more common nuts that can be dried are: Brazil nuts, butternuts, cashews, chestnuts, filberts (hazelnuts),

hickory nuts, macadamia nuts, pecans, pine nuts, pistachios, and walnuts. Your home-dried nuts will be nutritious and free from the preservatives found in commercial varieties.

General Rules for Dehydrating Nuts

Once harvested, nuts should be dried to a relatively low moisture content to store well. Afterwards, you can enjoy experimenting at your leisure with the many uses of this delicious snack and food addition.

Preparation. Nuts literally require no preparation. Just select ones with clean well-formed shells that are not cracked or broken. Old dried-out nuts will seem lightweight; heaviness is a sign of freshness. Either the whole, unshelled nut or just the kernel, or nutmeat, may be dried.

Drying. If you have mastered the drying method for herbs, then drying nuts will be a snap. Spread the nuts—shelled or unshelled—in a single layer on the dehydrator trays and place them in the unit. For best nut taste and shelf life, dry at 95°F. Unshelled nuts will take approximately 10 to 14 hours to dry; shelled nuts should be dry in 8 to 12 hours.

Testing. Shelled nuts are dry when the meats have become somewhat crunchy. However when cracked open, the nutmeat of unshelled varieties should still be tender. Dried unshelled nuts should contain 7 to 8% moisture, and shelled ones 3 to 5% for the best storage life. But, when storing dried shelled nuts, remember that no matter what container they are stored in, *they should be refrigerated.* This is due to the high oil content of nuts which make them turn rancid if not refrigerated or vacuum sealed.

Pumpkin Seeds. Many seeds, like pumpkin and sunflower seeds, are good snacking delicacies. Although not technically nuts, these varieties are used as such and have a crunchy, nutty taste.

Before drying, be sure to wash pumpkin seeds to free them of any pumpkin pulp. Dry at 110° to 120°F until crisp, stirring frequently.

Sunflower Seeds. Sunflower seeds contain about the same percentage of protein as meat and are also high in calcium, niacin, phosphorus, thiamin, and riboflavin. To harvest, pick or shake the seeds from the matured flower heads. Dry at 100°F until crunchy. Recommended varieties for seed production include Mammoth Russian, Gray Stripe, and Manchurian.

Peanuts. Though nearly always considered a nut, peanuts are actually a member of the legume family which includes peas and beans. Peanuts are higher in protein than true nuts, but they have considerably low starch and water contents. Dry shelled or unshelled peanuts at 125°F.

8

DEHYDRATING GRAINS AND DAIRY PRODUCTS

You've already dried fruit, vegetables, meat, fish, herbs, and nuts. What foods are left to dehydrate—PLENTY! There are various grains, breads, dairy products (yogurt and various cheeses), leftovers, and—if there is a small infant in the house—baby food.

GRAINS

Wheat, maize, and rice were being grown by primitive man long before recorded history. Drying grains and grain products is the most effective and practical way to preserve them for future use.

Dehydrating Grain

Wheat, barley, oats, and buckwheat should be partially stalk dried before being picked to dehydrate. The same is true for corn. Once the corn kernels are removed from the cob, spread them out in a single layer on the drying trays; other grains should be poured on in a 1/2" layer. Dry for 12 to 18 hours at 115°F. Dried corn should look shriveled. The wheat and other grains should be hard and crunchy with a nutty taste.

Grinding Your Own Grain

Why invest in your own grain mill? The nutritional value of fresh ground whole wheat is one good reason. The white flour milling process used commercially discards the bran and wheat germ which contain substantial percentages of the grain's protein, thiamine, niacin, riboflavin, pantothenic acid, and many minerals. Fresh grinding preserves the bran and wheat germ, helps eliminate the chance of vitamin deterioration, and lessens the possibility of the wheat germ oil becoming rancid. In addition, diets high in refined sugars and flours can actually be harmful. Doctors suggest that the addition of wheat and bran to the diet may decrease the possibility of cancer of the colon, heart disease, diverticulosis, and other related diseases.

Grinding your own grain saves money as well. The accompanying chart illustrates how much a family of five could save in a single year by using a grain mill.

Yearly Savings for an Average Family of Five			
Whole Wheat Products	Retail Store Cost	Stone Ground with a Home Grain Mill	Savings
1 loaf bread per day	$1.22 × 365 = $445.30	$.20 × 365 = $73	$372.30
One 15 oz box of cereal every other day	$1.57 × 180 = $282.60	$.06 × 180 = $10.80	$271.80
10 lbs flour purchased twice monthly	$3.30 × 24 = $79.20	$1.30 × 24 = $31.20	$ 48.00
Cakes and cookies baked an average of once a week	$5 × 52 = $260	$1.50 × 52 = $78	$182.00
		Total Savings:	$874.10

Operating a Grain Mill.   The grain is ground through the action of the mill's stone grinding wheels or in some cases is exploded into small particles by stainless steel micronizers. Quality mills have adjustable stones to vary the texture of the flour from fine for pastry dough to coarse for corn and soybeans. The mill itself may be operated electrically or through the action of a hand-turned crank.

To begin grinding, pour a cup of grain—wheat, corn, rice, barley, rye, or soybeans—into the hopper (loading area) and turn on the mill. The consistency of the flour can be determined by turning off the mill, pulling out the flour holding pan, and feeling with the fingers. The best whole wheat flour for bread is sandy, while pastry flour should feel fine. Because soybeans are oily, they should be dehydrated prior to grinding.

For breads, muffins, and other goodies you can make with your freshly ground flour, refer to the recipe section at the end of this book.

Grind dried corn into meal for use in breads, muffins, and mush.

Recrisping Crackers, Cookies, and Cereals

If your cookies and crackers have lost their crunch, put them in your dehydrator and revitalize their crispness. Place the cookies, crackers, or cereal in a single layer on the trays and dry for 1 hour at 145°F till crisp and crackling.

You can also make your own preservative-free crackers in your dehydrator. Prepare the mixture according to your favorite cracker recipe, place on the trays, and dry for 4 to 6 hours at 145°F. To preserve freshness, store the crackers in a tightly sealed container.

To recrisp cookies and crackers, place them on the trays in a single layer and dry until crisp.

Saving Stale Bread

Don't throw away stale bread, dry it into little croutons. Cut the bread into small cubes, place in the dehydrator, and dry for 4 to 6 hours at 145°F till crisp. If thoroughly dried, your croutons will keep for several weeks. For the zippiest taste, don't season your croutons until you're ready to use them in soups or salads. Experiment with interesting mixes of flavorings like onion salt, marjoram, garlic salt, Parmesan cheese, butter, and herbs.

Bread Crumbs.   Stale bread can also be recycled into usable bread crumbs. Place whole, stale slices of bread on the trays; make sure none of the pieces are moldy. Dry for 4 to 6 hours at 145°F till the slices are brittle and crumbly. When thoroughly dried, break the bread into small pieces, drop into a blender, and chop into crumbs. Bread crumbs can be used for fried chicken or fish coating or as a topping for casseroles and hot, open-faced sandwiches. When mixed with dried herbs, they can also be used in stuffing.

Noodles

Your dehydrator is perfect for preparing pasta. Store-bought varieties can't compete with the taste of home-made; you'll notice the difference with the first bite. For a delicious homemade noodle recipe, refer to the recipe section of this book.

Make and cut the noodles according to the recipe directions. Spread the strips in a single layer on the trays and dry until crisp. Dried noodles can be used in soups and casseroles; as a main dish buttered; or in a cream, tomato, or cheese sauce.

Raising Yeast Breads

Bread is the oldest food manufactured by man. Some of the many available bread recipes are given in the recipe section.

Remove the trays from the dehydrator and set the thermostat at 125°F. Allow the unit to preheat. Place a shallow pan of water on the bottom of the dehydrator. The bowl of dough is set on one of the trays, and the tray is inserted right above the water. To keep the dough from drying out, cover it with a cloth.

Allow the dough to rise for 1 hour, punch it down, and then transfer the mixture to greased loaf pans. It's now ready to bake to a golden brown in your oven.

Granola

Wake up to your own natural breakfast cereals. With your dehydrator, you can mix up a batch of tasty granola in no time. The potential combinations of ingredients are almost endless: untoasted wheat germ, oatmeal, sesame seeds, ground soybeans, sunflower seeds, coconut, peanut butter, almonds, graham, raisins, and other dried fruits. Lace them together with honey and vanilla, and you have granola.

To dry granola, cover the dehydrator trays with Teflex, kitchen parchment paper, or plastic wrap and spread on a thin layer of the mixture. Dry for approximately 1 to 3 hours at 145°F till crispy. Besides making a delicious cereal, granola can be fashioned into bars or cookies or layered with yogurt for a special treat.

Assemble granola ingredients and combine them in a large bowl. Spread the granola mixture on covered trays and dry to the desired crunchiness.

DAIRY PRODUCTS

Milk and eggs can be dried, but they require special techniques and equipment that are not available to most home dryers. Because there is a high risk of bacterial growth and possible food poisoning, the home drying of milk and eggs is *not* recommended. You *can*, however, use your dehydrator to make yogurt and cheeses. Due to the risk of contamination when making these dairy products, utilize these simple safety rules:

1. Wash hands thoroughly with a mild solution of detergent, bleach, and water.

2. Clean all utensils and containers with this same solution of detergent, bleach, and water.

3. Make sure all counter surfaces and bread boards are thoroughly cleaned in the manner above before contacting food.

4. After sealed containers are opened, use the contents as soon as possible. Store partially used containers tightly sealed and in the refrigerator to retard bacteria growth.

Yogurt

Residents of Middle Eastern countries have revered yogurt as a staple food for thousands of years, but it didn't really become popular in the United States until the late 1940s. Yogurt is low in calories and cholesterol and is reputed to slow the aging process.

Yogurt is extremely easy to make. All that is required is 4 cups milk, 1/2 cup powdered milk, and 2 tablespoons of plain yogurt. Use either whole, lowfat, or skimmed milk; it's up to you. For authentic Middle Eastern yogurt, you'd have to substitute goat's or sheep's milk for cow's milk. The yogurt, though, must be plain; there's no substituting. This means that it is natural with no additives and has not been pasteurized after becoming yogurt. Pasteurizing kills the culture, preventing the yogurt from being used to start new batches.

Making Your Yogurt. Add the powdered milk to the fresh milk and heat to boiling for a few seconds. The powdered milk gives the yogurt a creamier texture. Allow the milk to cool to 120°F; then take 1/4 cup of the mixture and stir in the yogurt. When it is thick and sauce-like, pour it into the remaining milk and mix well.

Spoon the yogurt into clean glass jars that have lids or into plastic yogurt cups. Place the containers on the bottom of the dehydrator, set the temperature for 115°F, and heat for 3 hours. (Using a higher temperature would destroy the yogurt culture.) If the yogurt has set, cool it. If not, continue to check the batch every 15 minutes until it does.

After the finished yogurt has cooled, add the fruit or flavoring before placing it in the refrigerator. If sweetening is desired, use powdered sugar or honey to maintain the thick, smooth texture. For a variation, blend 1/2 cup of fruit with 1/4 cup water and make a sauce to pour over the yogurt right before it is eaten.

Yogurt Leather. Prepare your "dehydrator-made" yogurt as previously described; then add jam, fruit, or fruit sauce and puree. You can also use prestirred commercial yogurt if desired. Yogurt leather is dried exactly the same

1. Nothing beats homemade yogurt. Combine fresh milk, powdered milk, and yogurt. Pour the mixture into individual containers and place in the dehydrator.

2. When the yogurt has set, add any fruit prior to refrigerating.

as fruit leather (see Chapter 4), but you can make an interesting variation by dropping the puree on the trays in spoonfuls rather than pouring. The result is little bite-size "kisses" that can be used as party candy.

Yogurt Facial. When making yogurt in your dehydrator, make an extra batch for a facial. The following facial yogurt recipe will help refine and clear your complexion.

1. Wash, rinse, and pat dry the face.

2. Apply mixture of 1/4 cup yogurt and 1/2 juiced lemon.

3. Leave this mixture on the face while bathing or for at least 15 minutes.

4. Rinse off with tepid water. (You may also rub a cut cucumber over the face at this point.)

Cottage Cheese

Cottage cheese got its name from the fact that it could easily be made in the home—or cottage. On occasion, it has also been called "pot cheese," because it needs to be kept in a container.

To make cottage cheese, you'll need: 1 gallon of pasteurized milk and either 4 tablespoons unflavored yogurt (the kind you made in your dehydrator can be used), 1/2 cup fresh buttermilk, or 1/4 tablet of rennet (an enzyme) dissolved in 1/2 cup warm water.

Pour the milk into a crock and warm it to room temperature, about 72°F. Mix in the yogurt, buttermilk, or rennet and cover the crock with cheesecloth. Place the crock in the dehydrator and hold the temperature inside at 85°F for 12 to 18 hours until clabbered. *Clabbering* means that the milk has separated to form thick, solid "curd" and watery, liquid "whey."

When the milk has thickened into curds and a little whey lays on the surface, the cheese is clabbered. Now your next task is to cut the curd as follows. Use a long-bladed knife and make all cuts approximately 1/2" apart. (1) Holding the knife vertically, make straight up and down cuts across the curd. (2) Now slant the knife and make diagonal slices down through the cheese following the cuts of step 1. Make the first cut at a 45° angle, but gradually straighten the blade so that the last cut is nearly vertical. (3) Repeat the process of step 2, only slant the knife in the opposite direction. (4) Turn the crock 180° and make a final set of vertical cuts to form a crosshatch pattern on the surface. This cubing process helps the sour whey to drain out.

The Final Steps. Place several inches of water in a large pan, set the crock in it, and heat to 115°F. Hold the cottage cheese at this temperature for 1/2 hour, stirring occasionally. Once the time is up, line a colander with cheesecloth and pour in the curds and whey. Allow the whey to drain off; otherwise, it will give the cottage cheese a bitter taste. To get rid of even more of the sour taste, dip the colander in cold water and gently stir the curds to wash away the last traces of the whey. Let the curds drain thoroughly. If desired add 1 teaspoon salt per pound of cottage cheese and 4 to 6 tablespoons of cream. After refrigeration, your cottage cheese will be ready to eat as is or in fruit salads, dips, cheesecake, and casseroles.

Cheese

The low temperatures of your dehydrator are ideal for ripening milk into cheese. Cottage cheese, which we've already talked about, is *unripened* cheese—that is, it has not been aged. *Hard cheeses*, on the other hand, are pressed, dipped in paraffin wax, and aged. Longhorn, cheddar, Colby, and Romano are all hard type cheeses. In addition, there are the *semi-hard* or soft cheeses:

Scamorze, Neufchâtel, and cheese spreads. These are generally milder in flavor than the hard cheeses and are only aged for a short time, if at all.

Cheeses have been made since ancient times, but most of these were mild and unripened like cottage cheese. If these old cheeses emitted a distinctive odor, it was due to spoilage rather than intention. About 900 B.C., however, cheesemakers discovered how to ripen their product and the trade suddenly began to grow in leaps and bounds. The competition for new, distinctive types was so great that many of the recipes were—and still are—kept as trade secrets. Cheesemaking in this country began when the first cows arrived in the New World in 1611. But it wasn't until 1851, when the first cheddar cheese factory was built in Rome, New York, that the industry really took hold.

You usually think of cheese as coming from cow's milk. But did you know that the milk of goats, sheep, camels, buffalo, and reindeer can also be made into cheese? The kind of milk used will affect the flavor and texture of the cheese. Other variables include the method used for clabbering and forming the curd, the ripening agent, the amount of salt and other seasonings used, and the conditions of ripening—temperature, humidity, and length of time. Today, all variations considered, there are about 700 to 2,000 kinds of cheese.

Making a Hard Cheese. The following instructions are for making a "generic" hard cheese; to cover all the different types individually would require a book in itself.

Scald 1 gallon of milk and allow it to cool; making cheese in smaller amounts is just not practical. Add 1/2 cup buttermilk or yogurt to the cooled milk and stir well for 2 minutes. Buttermilk and yogurt act as *starters*, substances that produce the acid needed to give cheese its distinctive flavor. In addition to giving the cheese its flavor, the acid also discourages the growth of bacteria. Set the thermostat on your dehydrator for 90°F, remove the trays, place the container of milk on the bottom of the unit, and heat for 12 to 24 hours. When the milk has a slightly acidic taste, it is *ripened* and ready for use.

Adding the Rennet. Enzymes in rennet speed the clabbering, or curd formation, of the cheese. Rennet is an animal by-product. If you are a vegetarian, there is also an all-vegetable rennet available. Allow the milk to cool back to room temperature; then add 1 teaspoon liquid rennet or 1 rennet tablet dissolved in 1/2 cup water. Mix well, cover the container, and let it stand for 1 to 2 hours until clabbered.

Cutting the Curd. Slice the curd in crosshatch and diagonal directions as described in the cottage cheese recipe. Return the forming cheese to the dehydrator, which you've set at 110°F. Hold the cheese at that temperature, stirring occasionally, until the curd is firm. This usually takes from 30 to 45 minutes. Test its consistency by squeezing a handful of the curd. If it breaks easily, the cheese is ready.

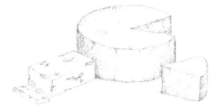

Draining the Whey. Line a colander with cheesecloth, pour in the curds and whey, and drain. Stir the curds with your hands until it gets a rubbery texture; it should squeak when you chew a piece. At this point, sprinkle on 1 to 2 tablespoons of flake salt and mix it in thoroughly. As soon as the salt has dissolved and the curds have cooled to 85°F, pour the mixture into a cheeseform that has been lined with cheesecloth. You needn't buy a special cheeseform, though these are available; a 2 pound coffee can with holes punched in the bottom and set in a shallow container will do just nicely.

Pressing the Curd. Place a circle of cheesecloth over the curds and insert a wooden follower. A *follower* is a circle of 1/2" plywood cut to fit inside the form; it serves to evenly flatten the top of the cheese. If you glue a small block of wood to the top of the follower, it will be much easier to remove. Now place a 1 pound coffee can, open side down, on top of the follower and set a board on top of that—forming a pyramid-type arrangement. The small can should protrude up several inches higher than the top of the form.

With all the paraphernalia in place, pile 3 or 4 bricks on top of the board. These will press and compact the loose curds into the familiar solid cheese round you see in stores. After 10 minutes, remove the bricks, board, can, and follower, and drain off any whey that has collected in the form. Replace the follower and other parts, increase the weight to 6 to 8 bricks, and press the cheese for an additional hour.

Dressing. Remove the newly pressed cheese from the form and peel off the cheesecloth. Dip the cheese in warm water to remove any lingering fat and smooth over small holes and cracks with your fingers.

Cut two cheesecloth circles slightly larger than the cheese round and a strip 2" wider and long enough to wrap around the cheese with a slight overlap. Roll up the cheese, place it in the form, and press with 6 to 8 bricks for a final 18 to 24 hours.

Drying and Paraffining. Remove the cheese from the form for the last time and wipe it with a dry cloth. Next, wash the cheese in hot water and smooth over cracks and holes with your fingers. The cheese is now ready to begin the drying phase. Place it on a shelf in a cool, dry place—the crisper or vegetable drawer of your refrigerator is a good spot that is also free from insects and pests. Turn and wipe the cheese daily for a period of 3 to 5 days until the rind—the hard outer covering—has started to form.

For better preservation, the cheese must be paraffined before it is stored any longer. Heat 1/2 pound of paraffin wax to 210°F in a pie pan deeper than half the height of the cheese round. Always heat wax in a double boiler type arrangement over water; heated directly, it may take on a burned smell. When the wax is hot, dip in half the cheese for approximately 10 seconds, remove, and allow the paraffin to harden. Complete the job by dipping the other half of the cheese in the hot paraffin and allowing to dry.

Curing. Most cheese will improve in flavor for several months. After a month, sample the cheese and reseal it if it is not ready. If mold develops, scrape off the moldy parts, rub with salt, and reseal. Date your cheeses, making a note of any special method used so that you can develop your own recipes.

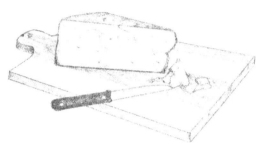

OTHER FOOD USES

There are several other food uses for your dehydrator that really don't fall under any of the categories we've mentioned thus far. No matter what you're dealing with, there are always a few square pegs that refuse to fit in the round holes. So rather than force them in place, here is each in its own category.

Dehydrating Leftovers

Dehydrate leftovers that would otherwise remain stored away and forgotten in the refrigerator; it's easy and economical. Virtually any liquid or solid leftover can be dehydrated and its usefulness extended. However, do not attempt to dry those that are already limp or on the verge of spoiling. Consult the appropriate chapters in this book for specific dehydrating instructions for individual foods.

Add dehydrated leftover vegetables to stews and casseroles, or rehydrate them and use as a side dish. Mix leftovers with herbs and spices, dehydrate, and you can create flavorful, nourishing soup packets to take camping, backpacking, or vacationing. When drying vegetables prepared in a sauce or syrup, drain before placing on the trays.

Dehydrate leftover canned fruit in slice form or puree to make leather. Dried leftover fruit can be eaten as is for a snack or added to cereals, ice cream, or baked goods. Rehydrate and puree leftover fruit for sauces and toppings.

Treat leftover meats according to the instructions for dried cooked meat found in Chapter 6. Chicken, turkey,

ham, beef, venison, and shrimp can all be dehydrated. Rehydrate meat leftovers for sandwich spreads, sauces, casseroles, and soups.

Make your own pizza and salad toppings from leftover cheese; Parmesan, Romano, and Provolone are all excellent when dried. Cut cheese into 1/4" to 1/2" slices or grate. Cover the trays with a layer of paper toweling to absorb the cheese fat and spread on the cheese in a single layer. Dehydrate at 120°F for 6 to 10 hours or until hard. Stir grated cheese occasionally and change the toweling at least once during the drying period. Pulverize or grate dried slices. Store in airtight glass containers. No rehydration is necessary to use the dried cheese.

Place liquid leftovers (like tomato sauce and soups) and even mashed potatoes on trays covered with Teflex, kitchen parchment paper, or plastic wrap and dehydrate as leathers. See Chapter 4 for complete instructions. When dry, your leather "leftovers" can be broken into small pieces or powdered. Store in airtight jars until ready to use.

Decrystallizing Honey

Honey stored for a long time may crystallize into a hard, solid mass. To liquefy it for use, place the container in the dehydrator for 2 to 3 hours at 110°F until no crystals remain. This process will not affect the taste or nutritional value of the honey; it'll be as good as fresh.

Baby Food

You want everything to be the best for your baby, and that's why you should consider dehydrating and making your own baby food. It's convenient, nutritious, economical—and free from chemicals and additives. Plus, you can use nearly any dried fruit, vegetable, or meat to make it. Just chop the dried food, place it in the blender with a little water, puree, and you have an instant supply of fresh and nutritious baby food.

1. When making baby food, start with flakes or powders. Place either powder or flakes in a blender with hot milk or water, let stand, and puree.

2. Your freshly made baby food is nutritious—and free from chemicals and additives.

When making vegetable foods, use dry powdered vegetables for infants and larger flakes for toddlers. The smaller the dried pieces you start with, the smoother the consistency will be. Mix 1/4 cup flakes or powder with 1/2 to 3/4 cup water, hot milk, or formula in the blender. Let stand until flakes soften or powders dampen, and puree; that's all there is to it. This amount makes approximately 3/4 to 1 cup baby food, depending on how much liquid was added.

Place dried fruits in the blender, cover with boiling water, and let stand for 20 to 30 minutes before pureeing. Strain the fruit if it's for an infant.

9

MISCELLANEOUS USES FOR THE DEHYDRATOR

Your dehydrator can help satisfy your creative cravings, shortening the drying times for ceramics, dough art, or decoupage. It's a boon for the impatient! You can even use your dehydrator to dry photographs. Treat and wash as usual; then shake or squeegee off the excess liquid and place on the dryer trays. Dry until no wet spots remain. (*Note*: Dry only photographs that have been printed on resin-coated stock; other paper types will crinkle unless pressed flat.)

Cake Decorating

Your dehydrator-dried cake decorations will look so professional even your baker won't know for sure; they're perfect every time. Royal frosting flowers will dry in 1 to 3 hours at 100° to 110°F. Piping gel and color flow designs will dry just as quickly.

Dried Fruit Decorations

Transform plain cakes and breads into culinary masterpieces with decorations made from your dried fruit. Dried apricots become glorious golden roses that taste just as good as they look. For each rose, you'll need approximately seven apricot halves. Place the halves on a piece of wax paper and roll them as thinly as possible using a rolling pin. Take one flattened half and roll it up in a tight cone for the center of the rose. Wrap successive halves around the center to form the petals; the natural tackiness of the fruit will hold them together. Slightly flare out the top edges to accentuate the petals. When decorating, add silk or candy leaves for the finishing touch.

Dried apricots aren't the only fruit you can use. Dried apple rings also make interesting flowers. Slice the rings open; then interloop them to form the petals. Add a cherry center, a cinnamon stick stem, and dried lime slice leaves. And where there are flowers, there are bees. Form your own bees by using shaped dried prune halves for the body. For the wings use fresh lemon slices; bend the slices under, and tie with string or thread to keep in that shape. Dehydrate as usual, removing the string shortly before the

Dried fruit flowers make any bakery item an epicurean delight. Delicate apricot roses were used to trim the bonnet cake; more roses, apple flowers, and prune bees decorate the tea bread packages.

slices are dry. To hold on the wings and attach other decorations, make a thick icing from 1-1/2 cups confectioner's sugar and 1-2/3 tablespoons of water.

Potpourri and Sachets

Potpourri is nature's own air freshener. With the right proportions of herbs, flowers, spices, and oils, homemade potpourri will remain sweet-smelling for years. In Victorian times, people grew fragrance gardens just for this purpose; the gardens included scented geraniums, thyme, lemon verbena, mint, balm, rosemary, lavender, and sweet marjoram. But you don't need a botanical wonderland to make your own potpourri; most of the ingredients can be found in your own garden or are easily purchased.

Choosing the Ingredients. Nearly any garden blossoms, leaves, or cones can be used for potpourri. Roses and citrus blossoms are noted for their aroma, while daisies, cornflowers, and baby's breath add color and bulk. As far as herbs and spices go, most can be found in your kitchen. (You can dry your own as described in Chapter 7.)

Bay leaves, cinnamon, ginger, vanilla, and white pepper are all favorites.

Fixatives must be added to the potpourri to prevent the fragrances from evaporating. Orris and benzoin should be available from a drugstore; other common fixatives are calamus and oak moss. The fourth ingredient, flavoring oils, can usually be purchased from a craft supply shop or catalog.

Preparation.   Start gathering and drying the ingredients for your potpourri during the summer months. This is the time when aromatic herbs are at their peak and flowers are their most dazzling and fragrant. Using scissors—never pull—cut only unblemished herbs and flower heads; one decaying leaf or petal can destroy a whole potpourri.

Spread the petals or herbs sparsely over the drying trays. Try to avoid drying both at the same time to prevent the distinctive fragrances from mixing. Dry for 6 to 8 hours at 110°F until dry and brittle. When cool, store them in air-tight containers in a cool, dark place until you are ready to assemble the potpourri.

Making the Potpourri.   For your potpourri, use the following general proportions of ingredients: 1 quart (4 handfuls) of herbs and flowers, 1 to 2 tablespoons of mixed spices, and 1 to 2 tablespoons of fixative. If adding a flower oil, use it sparingly to avoid concealing the other aromas (3 to 5 drops is more than enough).

Place the dried flowers and herbs in a large glass or stainless steel bowl and toss them gently with your hands to mix. In a separate small glass dish, combine the spices, fixative, and flower oil and blend well. Take the combined spices and sprinkle them evenly over the flower mix, gently crushing some of the herbs as you do.

Storing.   Pack your potpourri loosely in clean, tightly covered glass jars and store in a cool, dark place for approximately 4 to 6 weeks. Shake or stir the mixture with a wooden spoon one or two times a week. Once this "mellowing" period is over, the potpourri is ready for use.

Sachets are easily made from potpourri. Just cut out small, colorful material squares, sprinkle on some of the potpourri mixture, and tie with attractive ribbon.

When displayed in an open container, the potpourri must be renewed every few weeks. To do this, pour the mixture into a clean glass bowl, add 1 drop of flower oil, and sprinkle on 1 tablespoon of brandy. Hand mix the potpourri, allow to air dry, and repack.

Display.   Potpourri can be displayed in virtually any type of jar, bowl, canister, or container, from a wicker basket to a peanut butter jar. Use a large clam shell to carry out a sea motif or a classy cut crystal bowl or candy dish to add an elegant touch for a party gathering. Loose petals and herbs may be sprinkled in drawers or crushed and added to bath water.

Sachets.   Your potpourri mix can also be sewn into sachets to be placed in drawers and closets. In Victorian times, these were often attached to the backs of chairs and sofas so that the sweet aroma would waft around the furniture's occupants—setting the stage for long, leisurely romantic evenings. All you need to make sachets are scraps of fabric; bits of lace, ribbon, and/or cord; and patterns made by tracing cookie cutters onto heavy paper or cardboard.

Cut out the pieces with pinking shears; it prevents the edges from fraying and adds a decorative touch to the sachets. Allow two pieces of fabric for each ornament. Sew the pieces together, right sides out, leaving one edge open. Spoon the potpourri mixture into each bag, sew closed, and add a yarn loop at the top. Pack in plastic bags to keep the scent until ready to use or give as gifts.

POTPOURRI

1 cup rose petals
1 cup lavender
1/2 cup rose leaves, crushed
1 tbsp dried orange peel
1/2 tsp cinnamon
1/2 tsp cloves
1/2 tsp cardamom
1/2 tsp coriander
1/2 tsp tonka bean
1 oz orrisroot (fixative)

Collect and dry rose petals, lavender, rose leaves, and orange peel. Powder and mix together remaining spices. Combine spice mixture with the flower mixture and place in a large glass jar or crock. Stir all ingredients gently with a wooden spoon. Secure with a tight-fitting lid. Store in a cool, dark place for a few months, taking jar out once in a while to shake or stir. Individual sachets may then be made from this divine mixture.

Other potpourri recipes are given on pages 133-134.

Drying Flowers

You'll definitely have "flower power" when you start making your own dried flowers with your dehydrator. The controlled conditions of the dehydrator make sure that all parts of the flower dry quickly and evenly; there's no problem with molding, giving you perfect blossoms every time. It's the perfect way to preserve summer memories for those dreary winter nights when the trees are bare and the garden is barren.

Flowers tend to darken as they dry, so select ones that are several shades lighter than the desired final product. Roses, daffodils, daisies, and carnations produce some of the prettiest dried flowers. Yellow flowers will retain their color well, but many white ones will turn a dull, grayish brown.

Harvesting.   Cut flowers when they are cool and dry. The early morning, late afternoon, or evening are all good times. Do not cut flowers right after a rain or before the dew has evaporated. Although flowers in full bloom may appear the most attractive, they often lose their petals when dried. Those that are firm but only half open will stay together the best. To preserve as much of the true color as you can, flowers should be dried immediately after picking.

Preparation.   Pour a thick layer of silica gel—available at a florist's or hobby shop—into a container such as a shoe box. Or cover dryer trays with Teflex, kitchen parchment paper, or plastic wrap and pour the silica directly on them. Cut the flower stems to 1″ lengths and insert them right-side-up in the gel. Space them far enough apart so that the petals of adjacent flowers do not touch. Separate the petals into the arrangement you want using a toothpick. Once this is done, gently sift more gel over the flowers. Be careful not to crush them. Make sure the gel is in contact with all the flower parts; lightly tapping the container or tray will make the grains fill in.

Drying.   Place the container or trays in the dehydrator with a cup of water to prevent the flower heads from becoming too brittle. Dry for 6 to 8 hours at 110°F; then turn off the dehydrator and allow the flowers to remain undisturbed overnight.

Testing for Dryness.   Before actually removing any of the flowers, brush off enough gel from a few so that you can touch the petals. They should feel perfectly dry. If not, the flowers must be recovered and returned to the dehydrator for more drying. When drying different kinds of flowers together, test some of each kind. Each variety will dry somewhat differently. (*Note*: The silica will eventually become saturated with moisture. If the white crystals in the silica have turned to light pink, it is saturated with water. For reuse, heat the silica in the dryer until it has returned to its original color.)

1. Dried flowers have a variety of uses. Pick flowers during the summer months when they are the most fragrant. Always use scissors when clipping leaves or petals from the stems.

2. Spread the petals sparsely over the trays. Dry until brittle.

3. The dried petals can be incorporated into sachets and potpourri. Dry whole flower heads for use in flower arrangements.

Removing the Flowers. When the flowers are completely dry, gently tilt the container or tray so that the gel begins to flow off. As the flowers begin to peak out, slide two fingers underneath them and lift out. Lightly shake off any excess crystals.

Dry Box. Now pour 1" of silica in a metal or plastic container and insert the flowers so that just the stems are covered. This is called a "dry box" and helps to lengthen the flower's life. Cover the container with a tight-fitting lid and leave it undisturbed for 3 to 5 days.

Use. After the flowers have been dry boxed, they can either be used immediately or stored away for future arrangements. To store dried flowers, place them in a box of tissue paper to which 1 teaspoon of silica has been added and store in a cool, dark place.

When you're ready to make your display, take a small brush—like an artist's brush—and gently dust off any remaining silica. Stems can be made out of wire. Attach them by winding floral tape around the base of the flower, then down around the wire stem. To protect the finished flowers from moisture in the air, spray them lightly with hair spray or artist's plastic fixative.

Pomander Balls

These charming, old-fashioned aromatic delights dry quickly and easily when placed in a dehydrator. For each pomander, select a ripe, attractive apple, lemon, lime, or orange. You will also need 2 ounces of whole cloves and 1 ounce of rolling mixture consisting of 1/2 ounce ground cinnamon, 1/2 ounce ground allspice or nutmeg, 1 teaspoon powdered orrisroot, and a sprinkling of glitter.

Using an ice pick or awl, punch holes evenly all over the skin of the fruit and push a whole clove in each; the skin should be completely covered. Now roll the ball in the rolling mixture, thoroughly coating it. Let it stand in the mixture for several days, turning occasionally. Now arrange the ball on a Teflex sheet, kitchen parchment paper, or plastic wrap and place in your dehydrator with the thermostat set at the lowest temperature. Dry till shrunken and lightweight; then tie a long ribbon or cord around it for hanging. Or wrap in netting and tie with a ribbon or loop.

Dried Macrame Beads

With a little ingenuity, you can dehydrate vegetables for use as beads in macrame and other crafts. Before drying, make a hole in the vegetable slices somewhat larger than the cord or yarn groupings you'll be using for the project. Make sure the vegetables are very dry, with no hint of moisture. To use, spray with a plastic fixative, or better yet, varnish or shellac the beads to preserve them. Turkey neck bones and the "eyes" from ham slices may also be cleaned and dried to make interesting and unusual beads.

Dough Art

Dough art is a fun craft for children and adults. It's inexpensive and requires no special equipment beyond your dehydrator. Roll the dough, coil it, braid it, stamp it, or press it to make wall plaques, napkin rings, jewelry, figurines, small sculptures, and even Christmas tree ornaments. When dried in the dehydrator, the pieces become extremely hard, similar to ceramic clay. Try all three varieties of dough to find the mix you like best.

Salt/Flour Dough. Combine 4 cups flour and 1 cup salt; add in 1-3/4 cups water. (*Note:* The water amount may vary according to humidity.) Knead on a floured board 5 to 10 minutes or until smooth. The more you knead, the more pliable the dough will become. Roll out and shape into designs. Cover dryer trays with Teflex, kitchen parchment paper, or plastic wrap. Dry ornaments at the highest dehydrator setting until hard (approximately 2 to 4 hours). The thickness of the individual piece may affect drying time. Keep the dough mix in a tightly sealed zip-lock bag or plastic container; only take out what you can immediately use.

Glue/Bread Dough. Cut the crust off one slice of white bread, and break the white portion into small pieces. Add 1 tablespoon of white glue, mix, and knead until smooth and pliable. Using hand lotion on your hands to keep the dough from sticking, shape designs. Dry at the highest setting (approximately 2 to 4 hours). The thickness of the individual piece may affect the drying time.

Cornstarch Dough. In a saucepan, mix together 1 cup cornstarch and 2 cups baking soda. Blend well. Stir in 1-1/4 cups water, to which several drops of food coloring have been added. Cook over medium heat for 4 minutes, stirring constantly. Ready dough will have the consistency of moist mashed potatoes. Cover with a damp cloth to cool; then knead. Shape dough and dry at the highest setting (approximately 2 to 4 hours). The thickness of the individual piece may affect the drying time. (*Note:* Cornstarch dough will not keep as well as salt/flour dough and may mold.)

Basic Dough Art. To start with, you'll need a rolling pin, a board or work area, and a smooth-edged knife. Thoroughly flour the rolling pin and board. Place a lump of dough in the center and roll it out to a 1/4" thickness, flipping it several times. Turn the best side up and cover with waxed paper until you're ready to begin shaping.

Shape your dough pieces in one of several ways. One of the easiest shaping methods for a beginner is to make cut-outs with a cookie cutter. A round shape can become a sun, moon, ball, or face; a plain gingerbread man has the potential of becoming a whole cast of characters. Flour the cutter, press it firmly into the rolled-out dough, and wriggle to separate. Remove the cutter gently. Transfer the piece onto the dryer trays before doing any final shaping or decoration. Instead of using a cutter, you can also make patterns of your own on heavy paper or simply cut out the designs using a knife.

After you've gained some experience, you may want to try forming the pieces freehand. Roll the flattened dough into coils and balls and use them to build your pieces. (*Note:* Keep coils under 1″ thick or they may crack.) To form flat pieces, simply flatten the dough between the palms of your hands. Three dimensional objects made in this manner may require some type of prop or support during drying to prevent sagging. In the case of top-heavy figure heads, insert a toothpick down into the body portion to keep them straight. Finally, if you want to use the piece as a hanging ornament, place a piece of bent wire, a paper clip, or a hair pin in the top portion. Be sure to center it in the thickness so it doesn't cause the dough to crack.

Larger dough art pieces over 10″—candleholders, baskets, masks, plaques, mirror frames, or light shades—should be reinforced with another material. Chicken wire and aluminum foil are two possibilities. Dough art can also be formed directly on pieces of wood such as decoupage plaques. Just moisten the wood slightly before adding on the dough, and dry together.

Texturizing. Texture can be achieved in a multitude of ways. Just look around the house and you'll find innumerable items, such as keys, buttons, meat tenderizers, fabric, burlap, and combs, that you can stamp into the dough. Pasta shapes—wheels, shells, and curls—can be pressed into the dough and dried along with it. Or the dough may be pressed into a mold. To prevent sticking, coat wood molds with cooking oil and plastic or metal ones with flour. To create the texture of hair or fur, squeeze the dough through a garlic press. It's a great way to make Santa's beard or a little girl's curls.

Varying the type of flour used in the dough will alter texture and color. Instead of white flour, use whole wheat, rye, bran, or soybean. (*Note:* These doughs are somewhat more brittle.) Natural doughs look so warm and homey, you may even want to leave them "as is" and forgo painting.

Decorating the Pieces. The dough, itself, may be colored or the coloring can be done after the piece has dried. To color the dough, add one of the following before kneading: food coloring, tempera, spices, instant tea or coffee, colored inks, or dyes. Powdered colorings should be mixed with liquid before being added to the dough. If you intend to color in this fashion, keep the dough a little drier than normal to balance the addition of the liquid color.

Glazing should also be done prior to drying. A glaze is a glossy, transparent coating applied to the pieces to give them a "ceramic" appearance. Mayonnaise provides a wet, shiny look, while egg yolk mixed with 1 teaspoon water gives the dough a yellow-brown tint. Colored glazes can be made by adding food coloring to the egg yolk glaze.

Many people prefer to decorate their dough art after it has dried. Use any type of paint—oil, enamel, tempera, water color, or acrylic. However, acrylics provide the best protection for dough art pieces because they seal out moisture. Another way to add decoration is with acrylic-based molding paste. The paste is squeezed through a cake decorating tube to provide frosting-like designs.

Preserving Dough Art Pieces. All dough art pieces should be finished with some sort of waterproof seal. Varnish, lacquer, and shellac will all work, but they should first be tested on scrap pieces to see how they will affect the color. Probably one of the easiest sealants to use is plastic fixative, available in most art and hobby shops. Plastic fixative sprays on, dries quickly, and is usually available in matte, semi-matte, and gloss finishes.

1. Most dough art designs can be shaped with your hands alone; however, a garlic press is handy for making hair, fur, or feathers.

2. Once the hardened dough art has cooled, paint the pieces any way you desire.

3. Christmas tree ornaments are just one of the many exciting uses for your finished dough art designs.

Dips

YOGURT AND DILL DIP

1 cup oil
1/2 cup vinegar
2 cups yogurt
1 tsp dill
dried onion soup mix

Blend all the ingredients until smooth. Add 1/2 cup of one or more of the following: grated sharp cheese, crumbled blue cheese, chopped olives, chopped parsley, soy nuts, or sunflower seeds. Makes 4 cups.

HOT TUNA YOGURT DIP

1 (7 oz) can tuna
1/4 cup mayonnaise
1/4 cup yogurt
2 tbsp dried onions
2 tbsp dried green peppers
2 tbsp dried celery
1 tsp Worcestershire sauce
1/4 tsp seasoned salt
1/2 cup jack cheese

Soften dried ingredients by just covering with warm water. Add everything to blender and mix until smooth. Heat and serve with tortilla chips. Can be served as a main dish over warm buttered noodles or chilled as a summertime dip with fresh vegetables.

YOGURT AND CHIVES DIP

1 cup plain unflavored yogurt
2 tsp fresh chopped chives
1/4 tsp dried onions, powdered
1/4 tsp curry powder
1/2 tsp salt
1/8 tsp seasoned salt

Mix all ingredients in small bowl. Cover and chill. Serve as a dip with dried vegetables or raw vegetables, or use as a topping for baked potatoes.

PAPA'S CHILI CON QUESO— HOT DIP

1 to 2 lb cheddar cheese
1 large can green chilies
1/2 cup dried white onions, diced
1 cup dried tomato pieces
1 to 2 tsp dried red chili peppers
Red chili powder to taste

Reconstitute onions and tomatoes in warm water. Sauté onions and put aside. Cube cheese and add to pan. When melted add all other ingredients and gently fold in. Serve hot with tortilla chips. Leftover dip can be used as a spicy sauce for omelets.

(Clockwise from left): Fruit Cordial, p. 37; Yogurt and Dill Dip, p. 89; Corn-Tasty Chips, p. 90; Cheesy Crackers, p. 90; and Mushroom Turnovers, p. 91.

Chips and Crackers

CHEESY CRACKERS

1 cup dried wheat flour
1/2 tsp salt
1/3 cup margarine, room temperature
1-1/2 cups sharp cheddar cheese, grated
1/2 cup walnuts, finely chopped
1/4 cup dried onion flakes

Combine flour and salt. Using two knives or a pastry blender, cut in margarine and cheese. Stir in nuts and onion flakes. Form dough into a log. Chill in the refrigerator or freezer overnight. Slice into 1/4" wafers using a sharp knife. Spread wafers in a single layer on drying trays. Dry 8 to 12 hours at 145°F, rotating trays halfway through drying time. Makes 4 dozen crackers.

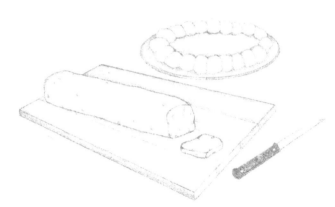

TOMATO-CHEESE WAFERS

1 cup cottage cheese
1/2 cup fresh or stewed tomatoes
1/2 tsp chili powder
parsley, garlic, onion bits, etc. (optional)

Blend cottage cheese, tomatoes, and desired spices into a smooth paste. Drop spoonfuls of mixture onto Teflex, kitchen parchment paper, or plastic wrap and dry until pliable chips or wafers form. Serve as an appetizer or as a complement to soups or salads.

CHEESE STIX

1/2 cup cornmeal
1-1/4 cups flour
1 tsp salt
1 tsp dried onions
6 oz processed cheese
1/4 cup shortening
1/4 cup water

Combine cornmeal, flour, salt, and onions. Cut in cheese and shortening until mixture resembles coarse crumbs. Add water, gradually stirring with a fork until mixture forms a ball. Take 1/4 teaspoon amounts and roll between hands to form logs. Place on ungreased cookie sheet. Bake in 425°F oven 6 to 8 minutes. Makes approximately 60 snacks.

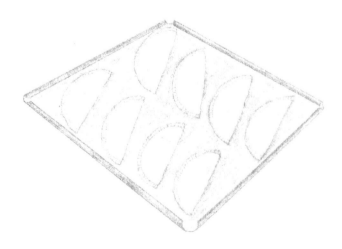

CORN-TASTY CHIPS

3 to 4 cups dried, powdered corn
3 cups fresh diced tomatoes or 1-1/2 cups dried
   tomatoes
1/2 cup chopped fresh onion or 1/4 cup reconstituted
   dried onion
1/4 tsp garlic powder
2 cloves (crushed)
1 tsp sea salt
1 tsp pepper (black, chili, or cayenne)
1 tsp dried parsley

Blend together all ingredients and spread mixture thinly onto Teflex, kitchen parchment paper, or plastic wrap. Dry until crisp. Break into chips and serve.

Miscellaneous

POTATO TOPPERS

1/2 cup wheat flour
3/4 cup cheddar cheese
1 tbsp toasted sesame seeds
1 tbsp bacon flavored T.V.P. (textured vegetable protein)
2 tbsp butter
1 tsp dried chives or green onions
1/4 tsp seasoned salt

Cut butter into mixture of all ingredients. Pat onto Teflex, kitchen parchment paper, or plastic wrap and place on dehydrator tray. Dehydrate at 145°F until crisp. Break into small pieces and serve over baked potatoes.

STUFFED DRIED FRUIT

8 oz cream cheese (room temp)
5 tbsp cream
1/2 tsp mustard
1/2 tsp dried garlic powder
1/4 tsp mixed dried onions
1/4 tsp celery seed

Combine cream cheese with cream and seasonings and blend. Place in pastry tube and fill with your choice of dried fruits, such as pear or peach halves that have been steamed 10 to 15 minutes. Sprinkle with chopped nuts.

MUSHROOM TURNOVERS

1 (8 oz) package cream cheese, softened
1/2 cup butter or margarine
1-1/2 cups flour

Mix together until smooth, shape into ball, and refrigerate for 1 hour. Thinly roll out dough and cut with floured 3″ round cookie cutter.

Filling

3-1/2 cups dried, minced mushrooms
2/3 cup dried onions
1 cup sour cream
4 tbsp flour
1 tsp salt

Add an equal amount of water to mushrooms; soak 20 to 30 minutes to reconstitute. Sauté mushrooms for 5 minutes, then add onions, sour cream, flour, and salt. Preheat oven to 450°F. Place a teaspoon of mushroom mixture onto one-half of each dough circle, flop over, and crimp with a fork dipped in beaten egg to seal. Prick top, place on ungreased cookie sheet, and bake 12 to 14 minutes until browned. Makes about 2-1/2 dozen.

SOUPS AND SALADS

Soups

CREAMY PEA SOUP

1 cup dried peas
1 tbsp dried, diced onions
1/2 cup dried carrots
1/2 cup dried potatoes
1/4 cup dried green peppers, chopped
1/4 cup dried celery leaves, crushed
salt
pepper
1/2 cup dried milk
3 tbsp butter

Put dried peas, onions, carrots, potatoes, and green peppers in pan and rehydrate in cold water. Simmer over low heat for 3 to 4 hours, until peas are soft. Add dried milk or butter and more water, if needed. Simmer, stirring often, 1/2 hour longer. Makes 4 servings.

ONION SOUP

1-1/2 cups dried, thinly sliced onions
1/2 cup butter or margarine
2 tbsp instant beef bouillon
4 cups hot water
1 tsp Worcestershire sauce
1/2 tsp salt

Sauté onions in butter or margarine. Try to use a casserole dish that can also be used in the oven. Add bouillon, hot water, Worcestershire sauce, and salt. Place in 350°F oven for 20 minutes. Remove from oven, sprinkle with Parmesan cheese or top with a slice of mozzarella, and place under broiler till cheese is browned.

CHEESE POTATO SOUP

1/4 cup dried onions
1 cup dried potatoes
1/4 cup dried carrots
1/4 cup dried celery
3 pieces rye or pumpernickel bread, cubed
1/2 cup cheddar cheese
2 tbsp butter
6 cups water
1/2 tsp pepper
1 tsp salt
1 tbsp dried parsley

Sauté onions in butter for 3 minutes. Reconstitute vegetables for 30 minutes in 2 cups water. Add all other ingredients, cover, and simmer 1 hour or until vegetables are tender. Serves 4.

CREAMY MUSHROOM SOUP

1-1/2 cups dried mushrooms
1/2 cup dried onions
2 cups hot beef bouillon
1/4 cup margarine
4 cups milk
1 tsp salt
6 tbsp flour
parsley for garnish

Sauté mushrooms and onions in margarine in a heavy saucepan for 5 minutes, stirring occasionally. Combine bouillon, milk, salt, and flour. Blend until smooth. Add to sautéed mushrooms and onions. Cook over low heat until the mixture comes to a boil, stirring constantly. Cook and stir 2 to 3 minutes longer. Garnish with parsley. Makes about 8 servings.

(Front) Beef Stroganoff, p. 99, with Homemade Noodles, p. 104; and (center) Creamy Pea Soup, p. 93.

HUNGARIAN GOULASH SOUP

2-1/2 lb chuck or round steak, cut in chunks
2 tbsp vegetable oil
2 tbsp margarine or butter
1/2 cup dried onions
1/4 tsp dried garlic, powdered
1 tbsp paprika
7 to 8 cups water (or any leftover broth)
1/4 cup dried green pepper pieces
1/4 cup dried red pepper pieces
2 tsp salt
1/4 tsp white pepper
1 tsp caraway seed
1 cup dried tomato pieces
1 small dried red chili pepper, crushed
1 cup dried potatoes, sliced

In large Dutch oven (5 quart), brown meat in oil. When browned, remove meat and set aside; skim grease and add butter to melt. Sauté dried onions and garlic until tender; then blend in paprika. Return meat to pan, add water or broth, dried peppers, salt, white pepper, caraway seed, dried tomato pieces, and chili pepper. Bring to boil; then reduce heat and simmer, covered for 2 to 3 hours, until meat is tender. Keep covered, and refrigerate several hours; fat will rise and congeal on surface. Remove congealed layer and heat soup again to simmer; add more seasoning if desired. Add potatoes and cook until tender, about 30 minutes. Makes 6 generous servings. Sour cream may be spooned over top of each individual serving.

MINESTRONE SOUP

1 cup dried navy beans
3/4 cup dried celery
1 cup dried tomatoes
1/2 cup dried turnips
2 tbsp dried parsley
1 tsp basil
1 clove garlic, minced
1 cup dried cabbage
1/2 cup dried peeled zucchini
1/2 cup shell macaroni
Parmesan cheese

Bring beans to a boil in 4 cups water; let stand for 1 hour. Reconstitute celery, tomatoes, and turnips for 30 minutes. Add parsley, basil, garlic, and 6 cups water. Bring to a boil and simmer 1 hour. Stir in cabbage and zucchini. Cook 15 minutes. Add macaroni; cook 15 minutes more. Serve topped with cheese. Serves 4.

VEGETABLE FISH CHOWDER

2 cups dried fish, chopped
1/2 cup dried peas
2 cups dried chopped potatoes
3/4 cup dried carrots
3/4 cup dried chopped onions
4 tbsp all-purpose flour
1 cup dried, powdered milk
1 tsp salt
1/2 tsp pepper
3 qt water

To use, reconstitute in the water for 30 minutes. Add spices, stir well, and simmer 30 to 40 minutes. Makes 8 servings. To take camping, combine all dry ingredients at home in a tightly covered container.

GAZPACHO

2 cups dried, chopped tomatoes
1/4 cup dried, chopped cucumbers
1/4 cup dried, chopped green peppers
2 tbsp dried onion flakes
1/4 cup dried carrot slices
1/4 cup salad oil
2 tbsp rose wine vinegar
5 drops Tabasco
1/4 tsp dried basil

Reconstitute the tomatoes, cucumbers, peppers, onions, and carrots in 3 cups water (about 1/2 hour); add the oil, vinegar, Tabasco, and basil, along with 2 cups water and blend until fairly smooth. Chill and serve with fresh sprig of parsley or cilantro and croutons. Serves 4 as a first course.

CORN-POTATO CHOWDER

1/2 cup dried corn
4-1/2 cups water
6 strips bacon
1/2 cup dried onions, chopped
1-1/2 cups dried potatoes, diced
2 cups nonfat dry milk
1 tbsp flour
1-1/2 tsp salt
1/8 tsp pepper

Rehydrate corn, onions, and potatoes in water; allow to stand for 30 minutes. Brown bacon in soup pot until crisp. Remove and drain. Brown onions in bacon fat until tender. Add onions to bacon. Place undrained rehydrated corn into soup pot, add 2 more cups water, and boil for 45 minutes. If necessary, add water to maintain volume. Add diced potatoes and cook till tender. Combine milk, flour, salt, and pepper with 2-1/2 cups water and mix well. Pour the milk mixture into the pot and bring to a simmer, stirring occasionally. Add onions and crumbled bacon; stir well. Serve with crackers or homemade bread. Makes 4 to 6 servings.

VEGGIE-BURGER SOUP

2 cups dried tomatoes
1 cup dried carrots
3/4 cup dried corn
3/4 cup dried peas
1/2 cup dried, chopped onions
1/4 cup dried celery slices
1/4 cup dried celery leaves
1 lb lean hamburger
1/2 cup elbow macaroni
6 peppercorns
3 beef bouillon cubes or 3 tsp beef bouillon granules
salt and pepper

Rehydrate vegetables in 2 quarts water for 30 minutes. While waiting, brown hamburger and drain well. Add hamburger, macaroni, peppercorns, bouillon, and an additional 6 cups water to the vegetables. Simmer until tender. Season to taste and serve. Makes 4 to 6 servings.

PICNIC BEAN SOUP

1/2 cup dried lima, navy, or kidney beans
1 ham bone with meat
3-1/2 cups boiling water
1/2 bay leaf
3 to 5 peppercorns
3 cloves
1/2 cup dried celery
1/4 cup dried onions
1/4 tsp garlic powder or 1 clove of garlic, minced
1/2 cup beer

Rehydrate the beans by soaking in an equal amount of water overnight. Combine beans, ham bone, water, and seasonings. Cook slowly for 2-1/2 to 3 hours or until beans are soft. During the last hour, add celery, onions, garlic, and beer. Remove bone from soup, chop meat, and add it to soup.

CHILI SALSA

2 cups dried tomato powder (add 9 cups water to make sauce)
1/4 cup dried celery
1/4 cup dried onions, chopped
1/4 cup dried green peppers
1 red pepper
1-1/2 cups sugar
1-1/2 tsp cinnamon
1-1/2 tsp black pepper
3 cups vinegar
salt to taste

Mix all ingredients together and cook until celery is soft. Makes approximately 3 quarts.

BEEF VEGETABLE SOUP

1 soup bone, with some meat on
1 cup assorted dried vegetables (corn, peas, beans)
1 tbsp dried parsley
1 tbsp salt
1/4 tsp pepper
1/4 cup dried celery
1/2 cup dried carrots
1/4 cup dried onions

Rehydrate vegetables in 1 cup water for 30 minutes. Cover soup bone with water. Cook 1 hour over medium heat. Pour boiling water over dried vegetables, just to cover; soak 1 hour. Dice celery, carrots, and onions; add these, the rehydrated vegetables with their water, dried parsley, and seasoning to the beef bone. Simmer 1 to 1-1/2 hours, remove the bone, dice meat, and return to the pot. Season to taste and serve hot. Makes 4 servings.

Salads, Toppings, and Dressings

HOT POTATO SALAD

4 slices bacon
1/2 cup dried, chopped onions
1/4 cup butter or margarine
1/4 cup vinegar
2 tbsp water
3 tbsp sugar
1 tsp salt
1/8 tsp pepper
3 cups dried, sliced potatoes
1 tbsp parsley

Reconstitute potatoes in boiling water; simmer 15 minutes. Chop bacon and fry. Sauté rehydrated onions in butter; add vinegar, water, sugar, salt, and pepper. Heat to boiling; then add potatoes and parsley. Heat thoroughly and serve.

SAVORY SEASONING MIX

3 tbsp dried onion flakes
1/4 cup parsley flakes
1 tsp powdered garlic
dash of cayenne pepper
3 tsp sea salt
1 tsp seasoned salt
2 tsp ground papaya seeds
1 tsp ground pepper
1/4 cup celery flakes
1/4 cup celery seeds
2 tsp dill seeds
2 tbsp paprika
1/4 cup poppy seeds
2 cups sesame seeds
3 cups grated dry cheese; Parmesan or Romano

Mix all ingredients together. Place in an airtight container and store in a cool, dry place. Sprinkle this seasoning mix over potatoes, casseroles, and salads. Makes about 1 quart.

SALAD TOPPING

3/4 cup roasted soybeans
3/4 cup dried onion flakes
1/2 cup dried carrots
1/4 cup each, dried red and green bell peppers
1/4 cup dried parsley
1/4 cup dried chicken T.V.P. (textured vegetable protein)
1/4 cup dried bacon T.V.P.
1/4 cup sunflower seeds
1/2 cup dried tomato flakes

Coarsely chop all ingredients in blender. Be certain all ingredients are thoroughly mixed. Store mixture in refrigerator in glass jar with tight-fitting lid. To serve, sprinkle mixture lightly over salads, casseroles, etc.

OLD WORLD HERBED FRENCH DRESSING

1/4 cup white wine vinegar
1 tsp salt
1/2 tsp granulated sugar
1/2 tsp dry mustard
1/4 tsp paprika
freshly ground black pepper
1 cup olive oil or other salad oil
2 sprigs fresh parsley
1 dill seed head (fresh or dried)
1 tsp dried basil
Optional: 1 tsp various other dried herbs such as tarragon, thyme, chervil, etc.

Beat the vinegar with the seasonings until well blended; then add oil and beat again. Mix in the dried and fresh herbs. Serve over any green salad.

LIME DRESSING

3/4 tsp dried, grated lime peel (or 2-1/2 tsp fresh)
1 tsp powdered dried limes
3/4 cup water
1 cup salad oil
1 cup olive oil
2-1/2 tsp dried and crushed red chili peppers
2-1/2 tsp ground dried cumin

Sprinkle a few teaspoons of water over the lime peel. Add the powdered lime to the water and let sit for about 3 minutes. Combine all ingredients in small bowl, mix well, cover, and chill. Makes about 3 cups of dressing. Serve over a cold shrimp, crab, or chicken salad.

(Clockwise from center right): Herb Butter, p. 132; Hot Potato Salad, p. 96, with kielbasa; Onion Soup, p. 93; and Raisin Custard, p. 121.

ENTREES

Beef

SAUTÉED SHISH KEBAB

1/4 cup dried onion flakes
1/4 cup margarine or butter
1/2 cup dried green pepper, in strips
1/2 cup dried mushrooms, sliced
1/2 cup dried tomato slices

2 lbs chuck or round steak; cut in 1/4" strips and marinate for a few hours in:

  1/4 cup Italian dressing, 1/4 cup soy sauce, or 1/2 cup dry red wine
  2 tbsp Worcestershire sauce
  1 clove garlic, minced
  Assorted spices: (pinches of) thyme, rosemary, onion powder, salt, and pepper

Cut meat into lean strips and marinate; drain well and reserve marinade. Sauté onion and peppers in butter until tender; then add mushrooms and sauté. Set vegetables aside. Cook steak strips quickly in (still buttered) sauce pan; brown on all sides. Return vegetables to the pan and add tomato slices and reserved marinade. Cook until thoroughly heated; add spices (and salt) to taste. Serve over rice or noodles. Makes enough for 6.

ZUCCHINI MEAT BAKE

1 small clove garlic
1 lb ground beef
2 tbsp oil
1/4 cup dried onions, diced
1/2 cup uncooked rice
1/3 cup dried tomato powder
1 tsp sugar
1 cup water
1 cup vegetable juice
1/2 tsp salt
1 tbsp dried bell pepper
3/4 cup dried, sliced zucchini
Parmesan cheese

Sauté garlic, onions, and beef in oil; then add rice (mix well). Add tomato powder, sugar, water, vegetable juice, and bell pepper. Cook 5 minutes; then add salt. Layer in pan with cheese and zucchini. Bake at 350°F for 40 minutes. Serves 6.

BEEF STROGANOFF

2 cups dried beef cubes
1-1/2 cups dried mushrooms
1/2 cup dried onions
3 cups beef bouillon
5 tbsp flour
1 cup sour cream
4 tbsp sherry

Simmer beef cubes, mushrooms, and onions in bouillon 1 hour until meat is tender. Remove from heat. Blend in flour, sour cream, and sherry. Return to low heat until sauce simmers. Do not boil. Serve over hot cooked noodles or rice.

(Front) Dragon Jambalaya, p. 101.

MEATLESS "MEAT" LOAF WITH MUSHROOM GRAVY

3 cups whole wheat bread crumbs, dried and finely
    chopped in blender
1-1/2 cups walnuts or cashews, ground in blender
3 tbsp oil
1/4 cup dried, chopped onions (plus 1/2 cup water)
1/2 cup dried, chopped celery (plus 1/2 cup water)
1/4 cup dried parsley flakes
1-1/2 tbsp tomato powder (plus 1 cup water)
2 eggs
1/2 tsp salt

Preheat oven to 350°F. Reconstitute tomato powder in 1 cup water; set aside. Separately reconstitute onions and celery in 1/2 cup water for about 2 minutes; drain well on paper towels. Sauté onions and celery in oil; beat eggs. Mix together the crumbs, nuts, onions, celery, parsley, beaten eggs, salt, plus tomato juice mixture. Spoon into a greased loaf pan (approximately 4″ × 8″). Bake for 1 hour at 350°F; cool for about 10 minutes before removing from pan and slicing. Serves about 8.

"Savory Mushroom" Gravy

1/2 cup dried mushrooms
2 tbsp dried onion flakes
1/4 tsp powdered garlic
2 tbsp vegetable oil
1 tbsp butter
1 tbsp flour
1 cup vegetable stock or water
1 tbsp soy sauce
1/4 tsp molasses
1/4 tsp salt
1/4 tsp dried savory
1/4 tsp dried thyme
pinch of pepper

Sauté onions and garlic in the oil and butter for about 2 minutes; stir in flour and cook (medium heat) for 2 more minutes. Add water, soy sauce, molasses, and mushrooms. Cook, stirring well, until thickened. Season with the savory, thyme, salt, and pepper according to taste. Makes about 12 ounces (1-1/2 cups).

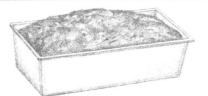

VEAL MEATBALLS WITH MUSHROOM SAUCE

2 eggs
1 cup dried bread crumbs tossed with 1/2 tsp poultry
    seasoning, 1/4 tsp pepper, and 1/4 tsp salt
1-1/2 lbs ground veal
1/4 cup dried onion flakes
2 tbsp margarine or butter
1-1/2 cups medium white sauce: 3 tbsp butter, 3 tbsp
    flour, and 1-1/2 cups milk
3/4 cup dried mushrooms
1/4 cup dry white wine or water
2 cups dried new potatoes, sliced or whole

Beat eggs; add the bread crumbs and seasoning mixture. Stir in the veal and onion flakes. Shape mixture in 1″ to 1-1/2″ meatballs. Brown meatballs well in heated butter; drain fat and transfer them to 2 quart casserole. Make the white sauce: melt butter, stir in flour, and add milk until thickened. Add mushrooms and wine (or water). Pour this mushroom sauce over the meatballs and dried new potatoes (potatoes may be arranged around the meatballs). Bake covered for 1 hour in 350°F oven; the casserole will be browned and bubbling. Serves 6.

Fish and Poultry

TUNA TREATS

1 cup (6-1/2 oz can) tuna packed in water, drained
1 hard cooked egg
1 small kosher dill pickle
2 tbsp dill pickle juice
2 tbsp chopped onions
1/4 cup chopped zucchini or celery

Puree all ingredients together in a blender; use a rubber scraper to push down ingredients until blended. Spread Teflex, kitchen parchment paper, or plastic wrap lengthwise over one dehydrator tray; paper or plastic should be taped in place at the corners. Spread mixture into a 9″ x 13″ rectangular shape, 1/8″ to 1/4″ thick. Dry 5 to 6 hours at 145°F or until tuna mixture curls and pulls away from the liner. Mixture may be pulled away from the liner and turned over during the dehydrating process. Break or pull off pieces as tuna chips for snacks. Makes 1 cup chips.

DRAGON JAMBALAYA

1/2 cup dried, chopped onions
1/4 cup dried, chopped green peppers
1/4 cup dried, chopped celery
3 tbsp butter or margarine
3 tbsp vegetable oil
1-1/2 tsp garlic powder
2 cups dried, sliced tomatoes
1/4 cup powdered tomatoes
1 qt water
1 tbsp dried parsley flakes
3 bay leaves
1 tsp thyme
1/4 tsp red pepper flakes
salt and pepper to taste
1 can flat beer
1 lb diced ham
2 lbs raw, peeled shrimp (Jumbo)
2 cups cooked, diced chicken breast
1 lb cooked crab meat
2 cups long grain rice
2-1/2 cups chicken broth or 1 bouillon cube plus
    2-1/2 cups hot water
1+ tsp turmeric

In large Dutch oven, add butter and oil and sauté onions, green peppers, and celery until tender; add garlic powder and simmer. Combine dried tomatoes and tomato powder in quart of water and rehydrate. Add this to the sautéed vegetables; next add parsley, bay leaves, thyme, and pepper flakes. Stir in beer, ham, and shrimp and boil until shrimp is done (no more than 3 to 4 minutes). Add chicken and crab, stir until heated through, and drain.

Rice

Pour chicken broth over rice and bring to boil; then add turmeric and continue boiling until steam holes appear. Reduce heat and simmer 15 minutes. Serve meat in center of platter and make a ring of rice.
Note: Special thanks to Captain Robert H. Stout, Master of the Yacht Dragon.

TURKEY TETRAZZINI

2 cups spaghetti, broken in small pieces
2 cups dried, cooked chicken or turkey
1/2 cup dried, chopped green peppers
1/2 cup dried, chopped onions
1 cup white sauce
1/4 cup dried mushrooms
1 cup chicken or turkey broth
1/2 tsp salt
dash pepper
1-3/4 cups grated cheddar cheese

Rehydrate peppers and onions in 1 cup hot water. Meanwhile, cook spaghetti. Drain and place in 9″ × 12″ × 13″ baking dish or 2 quart casserole. Drain green peppers and onions; mix together with chicken or turkey, white sauce, mushrooms, broth, salt, pepper, and 1-1/4 cups grated cheese. Pour over cooked spaghetti, and sprinkle 1/2 cup grated cheese over top. Bake at 350°F for 45 minutes.

JUDY'S BROCCOLI CASSEROLE

2 cups chicken, diced
1/4 cup butter
1/2 cup flour
salt to taste
1 cup milk
2 cups chicken broth
1 cup mayonnaise
1 tsp lemon juice
1 cup dried broccoli pieces
1/2 cup dried mushrooms, sliced
1 cup buttered bread crumbs
2 cups cooked rice

Reconstitute broccoli in warm water. Steam until a bright green color and just until tender. Set aside. Combine butter, flour, salt, milk, and broth; cook until thickened. Add mayonnaise and lemon juice. Put rice in buttered 9″ × 12″ pan; top with broccoli and mushrooms. Combine chicken with sauce, and pour over casserole. Top with bread crumbs. Bake at 350°F till brown. Serves 8 to 10.

KIP'S CHICKEN CREPES

1/2 cup diced dried chicken or turkey
1/2 cup dried spinach
1-1/2 cups medium white sauce
1/4 cup cracker or bread crumbs
1/4 cup Parmesan cheese
2 tbsp dried green onions
1/4 tsp crushed dried fennel seeds

Reconstitute meat in 1 cup hot water until tender. Drain. Reconstitute spinach and onions in 1/2 cup water until tender. (Drain any excess liquid.) Combine meat, spinach, onions, and bread crumbs; spoon into crepes; and roll. Arrange, seam side down, in a buttered baking dish. Mix cheese and fennel seeds with white sauce and pour over crepes. Bake at 350°F approximately 30 minutes.

Crepe Pancakes

1 egg
1 cup milk
1 tbsp melted butter
1 cup flour

Lightly grease 6" skillet. Pour 2 tablespoons batter in pan. Tilt pan until batter spreads evenly. Return pan to heat and brown on one side only. Repeat with rest of batter. Crepes can be filled with meat, vegetables, or fruit.

Pork and Lamb

PORK CHOPS AND APPLE

Rehydrate dried apple rings by soaking 1 hour, or until soft, in just enough boiling water to cover. Brown pork chops, season, and pour off grease. If done in an iron kettle, this may be put in the oven; otherwise, transfer chops to a casserole large enough to arrange them one layer deep. Cover chops with apple slices; add water in which apples were soaked and enough more to barely cover chops. Bake at 350°F for 35 to 40 minutes.

SWEET AND SOUR HAM

1-1/4 cups cubed ham
2 tbsp shortening
1/4 cup dried onion pieces
1 tbsp dried green peppers
1/2 cup dried pineapple pieces
2 tbsp vinegar
1 tbsp soy sauce
1 tsp salt
1 tbsp cornstarch
1 cup water

Reconstitute onions, peppers, and pineapples in warm water, just to cover. Drain. Brown ham in shortening; then add onions and green peppers. Cook until tender; add pineapple, vinegar, soy sauce, and salt. Mix cornstarch and water; add to meat mixture. Bring to a boil and simmer for 45 minutes. Serve over rice. Makes 4 servings.

DRIED HAM IN RICE

1/2 cup dried ham pieces
1 qt boiling water
1 cup uncooked rice
2 tbsp dried, grated carrots
2 tbsp dried, chopped celery
1 tbsp butter or margarine
2 chicken flavored bouillon cubes
1/2 cup boiling water
1 tsp soy sauce
1 tbsp chopped chives

Simmer dried ham in water over low heat for approximately 1 hour, or until tender. Add water to make 3 cups. Bring to a boil; then add rice, dried carrots, dried celery, and butter or margarine. Bring to a boil again, lower heat, cover, and cook 20 minutes without lifting lid. Dissolve bouillon cubes in 1/2 cup boiling water. Stir in soy sauce and add to cooked rice mixture. Mix lightly, put in a serving dish, and top with chives. Makes 6 to 8 servings.

HERBED LAMB

1-1/2 cups dried lamb cubes
1/2 tsp dried garlic, chopped
1/4 cup dried onions, chopped
1 dried bay leaf
1/2 tsp dried basil
1/2 tsp dried oregano
1/4 tsp dried rosemary
6 peppercorns
4 cups boiling water
1 cup dried carrots
1 cup dried onion slices
1 cup dried celery slices
1/2 cup dried tomato slices
1/2 cup dried peas
1/2 cup white wine
6 medium potatoes, cut in 1″ cubes
1/4 cup cornstarch
1/4 cup water
salt

Combine dried lamb cubes, herbs, seasonings, and boiling water in a large pan. Cover and simmer over low heat for 1 hour or until lamb is tender. Add dried vegetables and cook 30 minutes longer. Add potatoes and wine and cook 20 minutes more or until potatoes are tender. Remove bay leaf and peppercorns. Combine cornstarch and water in a cup. Move meat and vegetables to a serving dish with a slotted spoon. Add cornstarch mixture to liquid in pan and cook, stirring constantly until thickened. Season to taste with salt and pour over meat and vegetables. Makes 6 servings.

Side Dishes

GLAZED CARROTS

1 cup dried carrots
2 cups water
1 tbsp butter
1 tbsp brown sugar
dash of salt

Rehydrate carrots in water for 1 hour. Steam a few minutes until tender and drain. In another saucepan add 1 tablespoon water, butter, brown sugar, and salt. Cook for 2 minutes. Pour mixture over cooked carrots and gently rotate pan until coated. Serves 4.

CORN FRITTERS

2 eggs, beaten
1 cup flour
1 tbsp sugar
pinch salt
1 cup milk
1 heaping tsp baking powder
2 cups dried corn

Rehydrate dried corn in 2 cups boiling water for 1 hour; drain any excess water. Combine dry ingredients with eggs and milk. Add rehydrated corn. Drop from a tablespoon into hot fat. Fry until puffy and golden brown. Drain on paper towels. Try other dried vegetables like zucchini, peppers, or onion rings (but don't rehydrate).

CREAMED CORN

1 cup dried corn
4 cups boiling water
1 tsp sugar
1/2 cup cream
1 tbsp butter
1/2 tsp salt
1/4 tsp pepper

Add dried corn to boiling water; allow to stand for 20 minutes. Simmer corn until tender, approximately 1 hour. Drain off excess water. Add sugar, cream, butter, salt, and pepper to the drained corn. Bring mixture to a simmer, stirring frequently. Reheat and serve. Makes 6 servings.

SWEET POTATO RUB

1-1/2 cups dried sweet potatoes
1 stick butter
1/2 cup corn syrup
1/2 cup dark brown sugar
1 tsp vanilla
1/2 tsp cinnamon

Reconstitute potatoes in 1 to 1-1/2 cups warm water for 1 hour. Steam until tender. Mix with butter and beat until fluffy. Add syrup, sugar, vanilla, and cinnamon. Pour into greased baking dish and top with pecans or marshmallows. Bake at 350°F for 40 minutes. Makes 4 servings.

CREAMY MUSHROOMS

1-1/4 cups dried mushrooms, sliced
2 tbsp butter
1 tbsp dried white onions, diced
1 tbsp dried green onions
1 tbsp flour
1/2 cup cream
1 tbsp cream sherry
salt and pepper to taste

Reconstitute mushrooms and onions by covering with 1 cup warm water. Let stand for 15 minutes. Drain. Heat butter in skillet; add mushrooms, onions, salt, and pepper. Add cream; sprinkle with flour and simmer for 15 minutes, stirring constantly. Add sherry and serve. This sauce is an elegant addition to omelets, beef, and veal or spooned into pastry shells.

SEASONED VEGETABLE BATTER

3 cups dried vegetables (mushrooms, zucchini, onions, eggplant)
3/4 cup flour
3/4 cup buttermilk
3/4 cup milk
1-1/4 cups cracker crumbs
oil for deep frying
1 cup Parmesan cheese

Coat vegetables a few at a time in flour. Dip in buttermilk combined with milk and coat with cracker crumbs. Deep fry at 350°F for 3 to 5 minutes, turning until golden brown. Remove, drain on paper towels, and sprinkle with Parmesan cheese.

HOMEMADE NOODLES

1 cup flour
1 egg
1/2 tsp salt
3 tbsp milk

Blend all ingredients; knead dough by hand until stiff. Chill. Cut into thin strips. Spread strips in a single layer over trays, and dry at 145°F until crisp.

CREAMED POTATOES WITH PEAS AND BACON

1 cup dried potatoes
1/4 cup dried peas
2 slices bacon, fried and crumbled, or 2 tbsp bacon flavored T.V.P. (textured vegetable protein)
Sour cream and chives (optional)

Reconstitute potatoes and peas by covering with 1-1/2 cups boiling water. Steam vegetables until tender and add with bacon or T.V.P. to white sauce. For added richness, top with sour cream and chives. Makes 4 servings.

White Sauce

2 tbsp butter
2 tbsp flour
1/4 tsp salt
1 cup milk
dash of pepper

To prepare white sauce, melt butter, salt, and pepper in saucepan. Add flour and blend until smooth. Gradually stir in milk and cook over medium heat, stirring constantly. Mixture will thicken as it comes to a boil.

FALAFEL

1 large baking potato
1/2 cup dried parsley
1/2 cup dried onions
3 tbsp oil
3 cups garbanzo beans, cooked and mashed
1/3 cup sesame seed meal
1 tbsp plain yogurt
1/4 tsp powdered dried garlic
1 tbsp seasoned salt
1/8 tsp pepper
1 tsp paprika
1 lemon, juiced
pinch of cayenne pepper

Cook potato and mash. Sauté onions in oil, stir in parsley, and cook until tender. Add to garbanzo beans, and add all other ingredients. Mix well and form into patties using about 2 tablespoons of mixture for each one. Place on greased cookie sheets. Bake at 350°F for 10 minutes on each side.

SCALLOPED POTATOES

4 cups dried, sliced, or grated potatoes
4 cups boiling water
1-1/2 cups mozzarella or cheddar cheese, grated
1 cup milk
1 tsp celery salt
1/2 tsp dried onion powder
1/8 tsp pepper
1 tbsp butter

Reconstitute potatoes in boiling water. Place half of potatoes in a well-buttered 2 quart casserole. Top with a layer of cheese and cover with remaining potatoes. Add seasonings to milk; pour over layered potato and cheese mixture. Dot with butter and top with remaining cheese. Bake at 350°F for 1 hour.

HASH BROWN POTATOES

2 cups dried potatoes
1/4 cup dried onions
1/4 cup dried, chopped green peppers
salt and pepper to taste
2 tbsp oil

Redhydrate potatoes, onions, and green peppers, letting stand about 20 minutes. Drain. Add seasonings and brown in oil until tender.

HERBED RICE

1 cup white rice
3 tbsp butter
1/2 cup dried onions
1/4 tsp garlic powder
3 cups boiling water
1 tsp dried parsley
1 tsp dried thyme, or savory
1 tbsp dried sweet marjoram
1/2 tsp salt

Sauté onions in butter until tender. Add rice and cook until slightly brown. Add all other ingredients and cook 15 to 20 minutes. Rice should be tender and have absorbed all liquid. Serves 4.

Sauces

SPAGHETTI SAUCE MIX

2 tbsp dried onions
1 tbsp dried parsley
3 tsp cornstarch
1 tbsp dried green peppers
1-1/2 tsp salt
1/2 tsp dried garlic powder
1 tsp sugar
1/2 tsp dried oregano
1/2 tsp dried basil
1 cup tomato powder
1/4 cup dried, sliced mushrooms

Mix all ingredients and store in a tightly sealed glass container. To prepare sauce, add 3 cups of water to mix and simmer until thick. Serves 4.

TOMATO-VEGETABLE SAUCE

1 cup powdered tomatoes
1/2 cup dried tomato bits
1/4 cup dried eggplant
1/4 cup dried celery
1/4 cup dried onions
1/4 cup dried zucchini
1/4 cup dried carrots
1/4 cup dried bell peppers
3 tbsp brown sugar
1 tsp salt

Combine vegetables with 8 cups boiling water. Rehydrate for 30 minutes and then add sugar and salt. Simmer until vegetables are tender and sauce is thick. Serve over veal and top with Parmesan cheese or add beef or pork chunks and serve over rice.

HERB SAUCE

1/2 cup mayonnaise
2 tbsp thick yogurt
1 tsp crushed dried basil or savory

In a bowl, blend mayonnaise, yogurt, and basil until the mixture is very smooth. Use with tomato or vegetable soufflés and other vegetable dishes.

SWEET & SOUR BBQ SAUCE

1/2 cup dried pineapple bits
1 cup honey
2 tbsp cornstarch
1/2 tsp salt
2/3 cup wine vinegar
2/3 cup water, if necessary
1/4 cup dried green peppers
1/2 cup hot water
1 tbsp dried cherries
1/2 tsp dried peppers

Reconstitute pineapple in 1/2 cup hot water; let stand 20 minutes. Combine remaining ingredients (except water) in small saucepan. Cook slowly, stirring constantly until thick and clear. Add pineapple and sufficient water to obtain proper consistency. Makes approximately 2-1/2 cups BBQ sauce for beef, pork, or poultry.

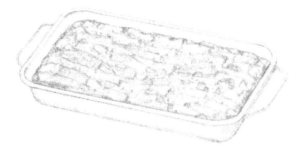

SPICY PIZZA SAUCE

1-1/2 cups dried tomatoes
1 (6 oz) can tomato paste
1 tsp dried onion flakes
1/2 tsp dried, finely chopped green pepper
1 tsp salt
1 tsp sugar
1/2 tsp oregano
1/4 tsp garlic powder
1/4 tsp grated Parmesan cheese
pepper to taste
1 bay leaf

Rehydrate tomatoes in 1-1/2 cups water. Combine tomatoes, paste, and seasonings in blender; add bay leaf and refrigerate overnight. Remove the bay leaf and pour sauce on each pizza. Add more cheese and other toppings of your choice: mushrooms, olives, anchovies, sausage, or hamburger.

Casseroles

POLENTA PIE

2 tbsp dried, chopped onions
2 tbsp dried, chopped green peppers
1/4 cup dried, diced celery
2 tbsp oil
1/2 cup dried zucchini slices
1/2 cup dried tomato flakes
2-1/4 cups vegetable stock or water
1 tsp salt
1/4 tsp chili powder
1/4 tsp cumin
1/4 tsp oregano
pinch of pepper
1 tbsp dried parsley flakes

Preheat oven to 400°F. In large saucepan, sauté onions, green peppers, and celery in oil until rehydrated and tender. Add zucchini, tomatoes, stock, and spices and cook, covered, until almost tender; stir in parsley. Sift together the wheat flour, baking soda, baking powder, and salt; then add the polenta or cornmeal.

Cornmeal or Polenta Topping

1/2 cup polenta flour (or cornmeal)
1/4 cup whole wheat flour
1/2 tsp baking powder
1/4 tsp salt
1/4 tsp baking soda
1 egg
1 tbsp oil
1/2 cup buttermilk
1 tsp brown sugar
1/2 cup grated jack or cheddar cheese

Mix the egg, oil, buttermilk, and sugar together. Gradually add the dry ingredients into the wet ones and mix until well blended. Grease a 2 quart baking dish and pour in half of the vegetables; spread the polenta mixture over top and pour on remaining vegetables. (Polenta rises while baking, creating a flavorful crust.) Bake the casserole for about 20 minutes; add the cheese during the last few minutes of baking. Makes 6 servings.

GREEN BEAN CASSEROLE

2 cups water
1 cup dried, cut green beans
1 cup white sauce
1/2 cup dried mushrooms
1/4 cup cheddar cheese
1/4 tsp onion powder

Bring water to a boil. Add beans and cook to desired degree of firmness. Add sauce, without reconstituting, and onion powder. Simmer in saucepan until heated through. Or place in 1 quart casserole, top with bread crumbs or french fried onion rings, and bake at 325°F for 30 to 35 minutes. Makes 4 servings.

ZESTY ZUCCHINI CASSEROLE

1 cup dried zucchini (1/2″ thick slices)
1/2 cup dried carrots (1/2″ thick slices)
1/4 cup dried onion flakes
1/4 cup dried bell pepper chunks
1/4 cup butter or margarine
1/2 cup ricotta cheese
1 cup white sauce

Coating Mix

5 slices of bread, cubed and dried
2 tsp onion flakes
2 tsp parsley flakes
1/2 tsp garlic salt
1/4 tsp ground sage
1/4 tsp poultry seasoning
1/8 tsp pepper
3 tbsp vegetable oil

Barely cover carrots and zucchini with boiling water and soak for 15 minutes. Simmer white sauce and cheese in small saucepan until mixture is smooth. Make coating by mixing together spices and bread crumbs. Sauté onion and pepper in butter until rehydrated (2 to 3 minutes) and add in one-half of the coating mix, the cheese mixture, carrots, and zucchini. Preheat oven to 350°F and place casserole mixture in greased 2 quart casserole dish. Sprinkle the remaining bread crumb mixture over top; then bake for approximately 35 minutes. Serves 6. For variety, use eggplant in place of zucchini. Thick home-made soups can also be used, and sour cream, cottage cheese, grated cheddar, or jack cheese can be substituted for ricotta cheese.

MEXICAN CHILLAQUILLAS

12 tortillas
2-1/4 cups jack cheese
1-1/2 cups tomato sauce
1-1/2 cups cottage cheese
1/4 cup dried green onions, chopped
1-1/4 tsp dried hot chili pepper
1/2 tsp dried oregano
1/4 cup oil
1 tsp salt

Cut or tear tortillas into 2″ square pieces. Sauté onions in oil in a large skillet until soft. Add spices and tortilla pieces, stirring frequently until tortillas are soft and coated with oil. Mix cottage cheese and tomato sauce in blender until smooth. Pour over tortillas, sprinkle with salt, and top with cheese. Cover skillet and cook until cheese melts and sauce heats through.

ZUCCHINI AND RICE TORTALINI

1 cup uncooked white or brown rice
3/4 cup dried zucchini
4 eggs, slightly beaten
1/3 cup melted butter or salad oil
1 cup shredded cheddar cheese
2 tsp dehydrated onions
2 tbsp dried parsley
1 tsp Worcestershire sauce
1 tsp oregano
1 clove garlic
pinch each of thyme and rosemary
salt and pepper to taste
top with Parmesan cheese

Cook rice until tender. Reconstitute zucchini, just covering with warm water. Combine rice and zucchini with all remaining ingredients. Mix well. Turn into a well oiled baking dish (12″ × 8″ × 2″). Bake at 350°F for 45 minutes (until firm in center). Serves 6.

DAIRY

Milk

BANANA MILK SHAKE

1 cup milk
1/4 cup dried banana chips
1/2 cup fruit juice (optional)
3 tsp dried milk
1 cup crushed ice

Add all ingredients to blender except ice. Let bananas soften; then add ice and whip until thick. Makes 1 serving. Other dried fruits such as peaches, berries, or plums can be substituted or combined to create your own special drink.

BANANA-PEANUT BUTTER SMOOTHIE

3/4 cup dried banana slices
2 tbsp fresh ground peanut butter
1-1/2 tbsp honey (or 2 tbsp brown sugar)
1/4 cup cottage cheese or plain yogurt
4 cups milk
1 tsp vanilla
1 tsp maple extract
1/4 tsp nutmeg (or to taste)

Pour 2 cups of milk and the dried bananas into blender. Add other ingredients and blend until smooth. In large pitcher pour remainder of milk and the banana puree mixture and stir well.

STRAWBERRY FROSTY

1 cup dried strawberries
1/2 cup water
1 cup cracked ice
1 cup unflavored yogurt
3/4 cup milk
3 tbsp sugar

Reconstitute strawberries. Place strawberries, water, and ice in blender, and blend for 2 minutes. Add 1 cup yogurt, milk, and sugar. Blend until smooth.

APRICOT SMOOTHIE

1 cup milk
1 cup yogurt
1/2 cup dried apricots
1/2 tsp vanilla

Place all ingredients in blender; puree until smooth and thick. Add sugar or honey to taste. Serve immediately.

(Clockwise from right): Wheat Bread, p. 131; Camomile-Mint Tea, p. 130; Nonnie's Great Granola, p. 123; Corn Bread, p. 130; Scrambled Eggs, p. 111; and Hash Brown Potatoes, p. 105.

Yogurt

YOGURT

4 cups milk
1/2 cup instant powdered milk
2 tbsp plain yogurt

Add powdered milk to milk and heat to boiling for a few seconds. Cool to 120°F. Add plain yogurt to 1/4 cup of the boiled milk to make a thick sauce. Stir into the remainder of the boiled milk, mixing well. Empty the mixture into clean glass jars with lids or plastic yogurt containers and place on the bottom of the dehydrator. Set the temperature at 115°F. After 3 hours, check to see if yogurt is set. If so, cool. If not set, check every 15 minutes until it is set. Dehydrated fruit may be added for flavor just prior to placing in refrigerator to cool. The fruit absorbs the moisture and makes a good thick yogurt. One-half cup of peaches, pears, berries, etc. may be placed in blender and mixed with 1/4 cup of water to make a thick sauce to use to flavor the yogurt also. If sweetening is desired, use honey or powdered sugar. For an elegant treat, alternately layer yogurt and granola in a tall parfait glass. Top with dried cranberries; keep chilled until ready to serve.

FROZEN BLUEBERRY-YOGURT PIE

2 cups plain yogurt
1/2 cup reconstituted blueberries
1 cup sweetened whipping cream
1 graham cracker pie shell

Blend yogurt, blueberries, and cream. Spoon into pie shell and place in freezer for 4 hours. Transfer the pie to the refrigerator 1/2 hour before serving. Top with fresh fruit if desired.

STRAWBERRY YOGURT ICE CREAM

1 cup yogurt
3 tbsp sugar
1/2 cup dried strawberries

Freeze yogurt in an ice cube tray until it thickens to a soft mush. Remove from freezer; stir in sweetened strawberries. Return to freezer until consistency returns to soft mush, as before. Beat well, and freeze until solid. Almost any dried fruit or combination can be used. Makes 2 servings.

YOGURT COLESLAW

1 cup unflavored yogurt
1/4 cup mayonnaise
1 tsp mustard
1 tsp seasoned salt
1/2 tsp salt
1/2 tsp celery seed
1/8 tsp pepper
1/4 cup onions, chopped
2 tbsp sugar
8 cups cabbage, shredded
1/2 cup carrots, grated
1/2 green pepper, grated

Combine yogurt, mayonnaise, mustard, seasoned salt, salt, celery seed, pepper, onions, and sugar in a medium bowl. Stir until well blended. Cover and chill several hours. Combine cabbage, carrots, and green pepper in large bowl. Pour yogurt mixture over vegetables; toss lightly. Serve immediately. Makes 10 to 12 servings.

CHEESY-YOGURT QUICHE

1/4 cup dried onions, diced
1 tbsp butter
1 uncooked deep-dish pie shell
1/2 cup crumbled bacon
1 cup cheddar cheese
6 eggs
2 tsp dried green peppers
salt and pepper to taste

Sauté onions and peppers in butter, place into pie shell, and top with bacon and cheese. Mix yogurt, eggs, and seasonings. Beat until smooth; pour over bacon and cheese. Bake at 400°F for 25 minutes until firm in center. Serves 4 to 6.

FRUITED YOGURT LEATHER

1 cup plain yogurt
1/2 cup fresh or dried fruit
Honey or sugar to taste

Puree fruit and sweetener in blender. Fold into yogurt and spread onto Teflex, kitchen parchment paper, or plastic wrap. Dehydrate at 135°F until leathery.

Eggs

SCRAMBLED EGGS

6 eggs
1/4 cup dried, powdered milk
1/4 cup bacon flavored T.V.P. (textured vegetable protein)
1 tbsp dried onion, finely chopped
1 tbsp dried green pepper, finely chopped
1/2 cup water

Combine all dry ingredients. Add water; let stand 10 minutes. Beat with a fork and cook in a skillet in which 1 tablespoon butter or margarine has been melted. Makes 4 servings.

DILL DEVILED EGGS

6 eggs
1 tsp crushed dried dill
2 tbsp mayonnaise
2 tbsp cider vinegar
1/2 tsp salt
1/4 tsp pepper

Boil eggs 10 to 12 minutes. Cool, remove shells, and cut in half lengthwise. Remove yolks and mash until fine. Add dill, mayonnaise, vinegar, salt, and pepper. Blend well. Fill whites with herbed yolk mixture. Chill before serving.

DESSERTS

Pies and Crisps

RASPBERRY CUSTARD PIE

5 oz package vanilla custard or pie filling mix
1-1/2 cups dried raspberries
1/4 cup sugar
9″ pie shell

Prepare the custard according to package directions. Rehydrate raspberries by covering with and soaking in water for 20 minutes. Add the sugar to the rehydrated raspberries and stir until coated. Combine the raspberry and custard mixtures, blending well. Pour the filling into the pie shell. Refrigerate for 3 hours before serving, and garnish with whipped cream.

NUTTY APPLE PIE

3 cups water
3 cups dried apple
1 tsp vanilla
1/2 cup granulated sugar
1/2 tsp cinnamon
1/2 tsp ground nutmeg
1/2 cup chopped nuts
1-1/2 tbsp flour
1/4 tsp salt
9″ two-crust pie shell
1 tbsp butter

Combine water, apples, and vanilla and simmer until the fruit is tender. Add dry ingredients and mix well. Pour into pie shell. Dot with butter. Moisten edge of lower crust; place top crust over apples, flute edge, and seal. Bake at 400°F for 35 minutes. Serve warm.

STRAWBERRY CLOUD PIE

9″ baked pie shell
2/3 cup sugar
1 envelope unflavored gelatin
3/4 cup dried strawberries
3 egg whites
1/4 tsp cream of tartar
1/3 cup sugar
1/2 cup whipping cream, whipped

Reconstitute berries in warm water. Blend sugar, gelatin, and berries in saucepan and bring to a full boil, stirring constantly. Place pan in cold water; cool until mixture mounds slightly when dropped from a spoon. Beat egg whites with cream of tartar until frothy; slowly add sugar and beat until stiff and glossy. Fold strawberry mixture into egg whites. Carefully blend in whipped cream and pile into cooled, baked pie shell. Chill several hours until set.

STRAWBERRY-RHUBARB CRUNCH

1 cup dried strawberries
2 cups dried rhubarb
1/2 tsp salt
1 tsp cinnamon
3/4 cup flour
1-1/2 cups sugar
1/3 cup butter

Reconstitute rhubarb and strawberries in warm water. Place rhubarb and strawberries in 9″ × 9″ buttered baking dish. Sprinkle with salt and cinnamon. Mix flour and sugar together; cut in butter until crumbly. Spoon over rhubarb and strawberries. Bake at 350°F for 40 minutes.

113

(Front) Apple-Raisin Cookies, p. 119; (center) Candied Fruit, pp. 37-38, Carrot-Nut Cake with Cream Cheese Frosting, p. 116; and (rear) Fruit Cordials, p. 37, Snitz Pie, p. 114.

SNITZ PIE

1 lb dried sour snitz (apples)
1 quart cold water
2 cups sugar
2 tbsp cinnamon

Add water to snitz and sugar and cook slowly to a very soft pulp. Add cinnamon and stir well. Remove from burner and allow to cool. Make pastry of your choice and line pie pan with it. When snitz mixture is cool, pour into pie shell and cover with top pastry. Slit top crust so steam can escape. Bake at 450°F for 10 minutes, then 350°F for 30 minutes.

ZUCCHINI PIE

2 cups zucchini leather, broken into pieces
1/2 tsp salt
1 tsp allspice
1 tsp cinnamon
1 cup milk
1 cup sugar
2 eggs
1/2 cup evaporated milk
9″ pie shell

Place zucchini leather pieces in blender. Add water to the 2 cup measure, and puree until smooth. Add remaining ingredients and pour into unbaked pastry shell. Bake at 450°F for 10 minutes and then reduce the heat to 325°F for 40 minutes, or until done.

DONNA'S APPLE CRISP

2 cups dried apples
1/4 cup orange or lemon juice
1 cup sugar
3/4 cup flour
1/2 tsp cinnamon
1/4 tsp nutmeg
1/2 cup butter
pinch of salt

Reconstitute apples in warm water. Butter a 9″ pie pan and fill with apples. Sprinkle with juice. Mix sugar, flour, spices, and salt together; cut in butter until crumbly; then sprinkle over apples. Bake at 375°F for 40 minutes.

BLUEBERRY BUCKLE

1 cup dried blueberries
1 cup shortening
1/4 cup sugar
1 egg
2 cups flour
1-1/2 tsp baking powder
1/4 tsp salt
1/3 cup milk

Reconstitute berries in warm water. Cream shortening and sugar; add egg and beat well. Mix dry ingredients; add to creamed mixture with milk. Pour into 8″ × 8″ pan. Sprinkle blueberries over the top.

Topping

1/4 cup butter
1/2 cup sugar
1/3 cup flour
1/2 tsp cinnamon

Mix flour, sugar, and cinnamon; cut in butter until crumbly. Spoon over top. Bake at 375°F for 45 minutes.

HERB TART

4 eggs
1 cup milk
salt
pepper
nutmeg
1-1/3 tbsp ground, dried green onions
1/2 cup finely ground dried lettuce,
    rehydrated in 1/2 cup water
1 tsp crushed dried chives
1 tsp crushed dried basil
1 tsp finely ground dill weed
1 tbsp crushed dried parsley
1/4 tsp powdered dried rosemary
10″ pie shell, baked
powdered dried red bell pepper

Beat eggs and milk together in a bowl. Add remaining ingredients, excluding shell and red pepper, and mix well. Pour into pie shell. Bake at 300°F for 25 to 35 minutes, or until tart is firm but still jiggly in the middle. Garnish with red pepper. Serve hot or cold cut in wedges. Makes 4 servings.

WALNUT TORTE

2 cups walnuts
4 egg yolks
1/4 cup honey
1 tsp vanilla
1 tsp dried orange peel
4 egg whites (at room temperature)
reconstituted fruit leather
whipped cream

Grind walnuts, a little at a time, in a blender or food processor until fine. Beat egg yolks until thick and light; then beat in honey, vanilla, and orange peel. Fold in ground nuts. Beat the egg whites until stiff, but moist; fold a little of them into the yolk mixture, and then add the remainder. Butter a 9″ cake pan. Cut a piece of brown paper to fit the bottom, place it in the pan, and butter it. Gently pour the batter in the pan. Bake at 350°F for 10 minutes; reduce heat to 300°F and bake 15 to 20 minutes longer or until done. Turn out cake to cool and remove paper. Spread with reconstituted fruit leather and top with whipped cream.

NUTTY WHEAT PASTRY SHELL

1 cup whole wheat flour
3 tbsp butter, chilled
1/4 tsp salt
2 tbsp olive oil
3 tbsp ice water
2 tbsp dried pecans, walnuts, cashews, almonds, or filberts ground until almost like nut butter

Put flour in a bowl. Work in butter with a pastry blender or two knives until the butter is in pea-size pieces. In a separate bowl, combine salt, oil, and ice water and mix well. Stir into butter/flour mixture along with ground nuts. Add more ice water if needed to make the dough stick together. Press dough into a pie dish. Bake at 400°F for 12 to 15 minutes until brown. Makes one shell that can be filled with the mixture of your choice.

PUMPKIN PIE

2 cups pumpkin leather, broken in small pieces
3 eggs
1 cup sugar
1 tsp salt
1 tsp cinnamon
1/2 tsp cloves
1 can evaporated milk
1/2 tsp ginger

Rehydrate pumpkin by adding enough water to cover; let stand while assembling other ingredients. Place all ingredients, including rehydrated pumpkin, in a blender. Blend to thick custard consistency. Pour into unbaked pie shell. Bake at 425°F for 15 minutes; reduce heat to 350°F and bake another 45 minutes. Pie is ready when knife inserted in center comes out clean. Cool and serve with whipped cream.

Cakes and Bars

PLUM PUFFS

1 cup dried plums
1 cup boiling water
1/2 tbsp dried orange peel
3 cups unsifted flour
4 tsp baking powder
1/2 tsp salt
1/2 tsp nutmeg
1/2 tsp cinnamon
4 eggs, beaten
3/4 cup brown sugar
1 cup milk
3/4 cup sugar
1 tsp cinnamon

Combine dried plums and orange peel. Cover with boiling water and let stand for at least 5 minutes. Sift flour, baking powder, salt, nutmeg, and cinnamon together twice. Beat eggs thoroughly. Add sugar and beat till thick. Add milk and sifted dried ingredients alternately. Drain plums and orange peel, and fold into the batter. Drop by spoonfuls into hot oil and deep fry until golden brown. Drain on paper towels. Combine sugar and cinnamon in shallow dish; roll hot puffs in mixture. Makes about 4 dozen.

CARROT-NUT CAKE

2 cups boiling water
2 cups dried, shredded carrots
2 cups sugar
1-1/2 cups vegetable oil
2 cups sifted flour
2 tsp baking soda
2 tsp baking powder
1 tsp salt
3 tsp cinnamon
4 eggs, well beaten
1/2 cup chopped walnuts

Pour boiling water over dried carrots; let stand 1/2 hour to reconstitute. Drain. Mix sugar and oil. Add flour, baking soda, baking powder, salt, and cinnamon. Add beaten eggs. Then add carrots and nuts. Pour into well-greased and floured oblong pan. Bake in 350°F oven for 30 to 35 minutes.

Cream Cheese Frosting

1 (8 oz) package cream cheese
1/2 cup butter
1 tsp vanilla
1 lb confectioner's sugar
fresh carrot slices and raisins for garnish

For frosting, place cream cheese and butter in a medium bowl and beat until fluffy. Add vanilla. If frosting is stiff, add a little milk. Gradually add the sugar; beat until smooth and creamy. Spread frosting over cooled cake. Garnish with fresh carrot slices and raisins, if desired.

CANDIED CREAM CHEESE TEACAKES

1 (8 oz) package cream cheese
1 egg
1-1/3 cups sugar
dash of salt
1 cup candied fruit
1 box lemon cake mix

Combine first five ingredients; beat well. Prepare cake mix as directed. Fill muffin cups halfway with cake mixture and top each with a heaping spoon of cheese mixture. Bake at 350°F for 30 to 35 minutes. Makes 18 to 24 servings.

CONFETTI CAKE

1 egg
1-1/4 cups flour
1 cup sugar
2 cups mixed dried fruits, chopped fine
3/4 cup water
1 tsp soda
1/2 tsp salt
1 tsp vanilla
1/2 cup walnuts
1/2 cup brown sugar

Soften fruits in warm water. Beat egg; then add the next seven ingredients. Mix well and pour into a 9″ × 12″ pan. Combine brown sugar and walnuts and sprinkle over top. Bake at 350°F for 60 minutes. Top with whipped cream.

CHRISTMAS FRUITCAKE BARS

1-1/2 cups walnuts
1 cup raisins
1 cup pitted dates, cut in large pieces
1 cup dried candied fruit
1 cup flour
4 eggs
1 tsp salt
1 cup light brown sugar, packed
1 tsp vanilla
Peel of one orange, finely grated

In a large bowl, combine walnuts, raisins, dates, and candied fruit; sprinkle with 1/4 cup flour. Toss to coat and separate pieces; set aside. In a small bowl, beat eggs to mix. Blend in salt, brown sugar, and vanilla. Stir in remaining 3/4 cup flour until blended. Stir in the orange peel. Pour batter over the fruit mixture and mix well. Pour into a greased 15″ x 10″ x 1″ jelly roll pan. Bake for 30 to 35 minutes at 325°F. Cool in pan, cut into 60 bars or 36 squares, and dust top with confectioner's sugar if desired.

APRICOT-NUT BARS

3/4 cup soft shortening
  (part butter)
1 cup brown sugar (packed)
3/4 cup sifted flour
1/2 tsp soda
1 tsp almond extract
1 tsp salt
1-1/2 cups rolled oats

Combine all ingredients and blend thoroughly. Place one half of the mixture in greased 9″ x 13″ pan. Press and flatten. Spread with cooled filling and cover with remaining crumb mixture. Bake until browned. Glaze and cut into bars. Bake at 400°F for 25 to 30 minutes.

Filling

3 cups dried apricot slices
1-1/2 cups water
1/2 cup chopped walnuts
1/2 cup sugar

Cook apricots in the water; then mash. Add walnuts and sugar. Continue cooking over low heat until thickened. Cool.

Glaze

1/2 cup orange juice
3/4 cup powdered sugar
1/2 tsp grated peel

Mix orange juice, powdered sugar, and grated peel.

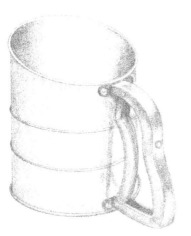

APRICOT-ALMOND BALLS

2 cups (1 pint) ricotta cheese
pinch of salt
1/4 oz honey
1-1/2 cups almonds
1 cup dried apricots

Cream together the cheese, honey, and salt. Finely grind almonds in blender. Steam the apricots for 5 minutes to soften; then finely chop. Add the almonds (only 1 cup) and apricots to the honey-cheese mixture; mix well and chill for several hours. Form into balls (made from 1 to 2 tablespoons of the mixture); roll each one in the remaining chopped almonds. Makes about 3-1/2 dozen.

BLUEBERRY-PEACH KUCHEN

1 two-layer white cake mix
1/2 cup flaked coconut
1/2 cup butter
1/2 cup dried blueberries (optional)
2 cups dried peaches (1lb 13 oz)
2 tbsp sugar
1/2 tsp cinnamon
1 cup sour cream
1 slightly beaten egg

Reconstitute peaches and berries in warm water. Combine cake mix and coconut; then cut in butter until mixture is crumbly. Lightly press into bottom and 1/2″ up the sides of a 9″ × 13″ pan. Bake at 350°F for 10 to 15 minutes. Arrange peach slices and blueberries over crust. Sprinkle with sugar and cinnamon. Blend sour cream and egg together and pour over top. Bake at 350°F for 10 minutes, just until sour cream is firm.

QUICK FRUIT DOUGHNUT HOLES

1 can buttermilk biscuits
1/2 cup mixed dried fruits, cut into small pieces
frying oil
sugar and cinnamon mixture

Cut each biscuit into four sections. Place one piece of fruit on each center and wrap edges around to enclose. Drop in oil heated to 350°F; turn over when golden brown. Drain on paper towels and roll in 1 part cinnamon combined with 4 parts sugar. Makes 32 doughnut holes.

Cookies

PERSIMMON COOKIES

1/2 cup dried persimmon pulp
1 tsp baking soda, added to persimmon pulp
1 cup sugar
1/2 cup butter
1 egg
2 cups flour
1 tsp cinnamon
1/2 tsp nutmeg
1/2 tsp cloves
1/2 cup raisins
1/2 cup chopped dates
1/2 cup walnuts
1 tsp vanilla

Reconstitute persimmon pulp in warm water. Cream sugar and butter; add egg, pulp, and vanilla. Beat well. Slowly add flour and remaining ingredients. Drop by spoonfuls onto ungreased cookie sheets. Bake at 375°F for 10 to 12 minutes.

BLUEBERRY OATMEAL COOKIES

1/2 cup shortening
1/2 cup butter
1-1/2 cups dark brown sugar
2 eggs
1 tsp vanilla
2 cups sifted flour
1 tsp baking powder
1 tsp salt
1/2 tsp soda
2-1/2 cups quick-cooking rolled oats
blueberry filling

Cream shortening, butter, and sugar until fluffy. Add eggs and vanilla; beat well. Sift together flour, baking powder, salt, and soda. Add to creamed mixture and blend thoroughly. Stir in oats. Chill 1 hour. Working with half of the mixture at a time, roll the dough out on a well-floured pastry cloth to a little less than 1/4" thickness. Cut with round cutter. Place 1 tablespoon blueberry filling on a half and cover with second half. Flute edges and pierce center top. Bake on ungreased cookie sheet at 350°F for 12 minutes. Makes about 30 cookies.

Blueberry Filling

2 cups dried blueberries
1/2 cup water
3 tbsp cornstarch
3 tbsp lemon juice
1/2 cup sugar

Combine all ingredients; simmer 10 to 15 minutes.

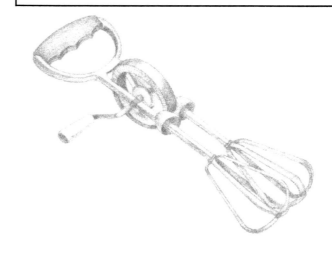

NORWEGIAN NATURAL COOKIES

3/4 cup chunky peanut butter
1/2 cup honey
3/4 cup wheat germ
3/4 cup dry milk (instant nonfat)
2 tbsp brewers yeast
1 cup raisins
1/2 cup chopped dried apricots
1 egg white (beaten)
3/4 cup shredded coconut

Beat together peanut butter and honey; add and mix well the wheat germ, yeast, and dry milk; then add raisins and apricots. Shape into about 1-1/2" balls; dip in egg white and roll in coconut. Makes about 2 dozen cookies.

APPLE-RAISIN COOKIES

1/2 cup butter or margarine
1/2 cup shortening
3/4 cup granulated sugar
3/4 cup firmly packed brown sugar
2 eggs
2-1/2 cups all-purpose flour
2 tsp cream of tartar
1/4 tsp salt
3 tsp cinnamon
1 cup coarsely chopped, dried apple
1/2 cup raisins

Coating

1-1/2 tsp cinnamon
3 tbsp sugar

Grease baking sheets and set aside. In a large bowl cream butter (or margarine) and shortening with the granulated sugar and brown sugar. Add eggs and beat well. In another bowl, mix flour, cream of tartar, salt, and cinnamon. Add to creamed mixture and mix well. Stir in the dried apple and raisins. In a shallow bowl, mix the sugar and cinnamon for the coating. With hands, roll dough into 1" balls. Roll balls in sugar-cinnamon mixture until well coated. Place balls 2" apart on prepared baking trays. Bake in a 400°F oven 7 to 8 minutes until edges are slightly golden. Remove from baking sheet and transfer to a cooling rack. Makes about 60 cookies.

SPARKLING COCONUT MACAROONS

2 cups moist coconut
1/2 cup sweetened condensed milk
1/4 cup dried berries
1/4 cup dried, chopped pineapple
1/4 cup pecans, finely chopped (optional)
1 tsp vanilla

Combine all ingredients except dried fruit and beat well. Add fruit and drop tablespoonfuls onto greased cookie sheets. Bake at 300°F for 18 minutes until light brown.

Candy and Fruits

DRIED FRUIT CANDY

1 cup mixed dried fruit, cut in 1/4" pieces
2-1/2 cups dried flaked coconut
3/4 cut sweetened condensed milk
1 cup finely chopped walnuts

Mix fruit with coconut and milk and shape into walnut-sized balls. Roll in nuts and refrigerate until firm.

ELEGANT CANDY CONFECTIONS

Dried fruits
Carob or semi-sweet chocolate pieces

Melt chocolate for dipping in a double boiler or microwave oven. Dip 1" pieces of fruit in chocolate to coat and place on a cookie sheet covered with Teflex, kitchen parchment paper, or plastic wrap. Let harden in a cool place (do not refrigerate). Fruit can be sprinkled with coconut or nuts or stuffed with cream cheese before dipping.

BOURBON STREET BON BONS

1/4 cup dried banana flakes plus 1/4 cup water (1/2 cup pureed banana)
2/3 cup granulated sugar
1 cup semi-sweet chocolate, melted
2-1/2 cups plain cookie crumbs, pulverized
1 cup chopped pecans or walnuts
1/4 cup light corn syrup
1/3 cup powdered sugar
1/3 cup cocoa (or carob powder)

Reconstitute dried bananas in water; puree in blender, adding the sugar as well. Melt chocolate. Combine cookie crumbs and pecans in large bowl. Pour in banana mixture, melted chocolate, and corn syrup; blend well with wooden spoon. Form this mixture into 1" balls. Combine powdered sugar and cocoa; roll candy balls in this sugar-cocoa mixture. Store in jar with tight-fitting lid. Makes about 48 bon bons.

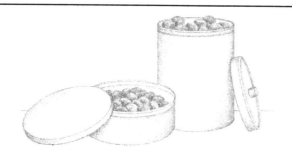

FRUIT FRITTERS

1 cup small pieces of dried fruit
1 cup flour
1 tsp baking powder
1/2 tsp salt
3 tbsp sugar
1 egg
1/3 cup milk
1 tsp melted butter

Reconstitute fruit in warm water. Sift together flour, baking powder, salt, and sugar. Add a beaten egg to milk and butter; then combine with flour and beat until batter is smooth. Fold in fruit (suggestions—apples, bananas, pineapple, or apricots). Drop spoonfuls into oil heated to 350°F. Turn fritters to brown on both sides. Total cooking time is 4 to 5 minutes. Remove from oil with a slotted spoon and place on paper towels. Sprinkle with powdered sugar and serve warm or cold.

TROPICAL FRUIT FANTASY

2 cups dried pineapple pieces
1 cup dried mango pieces
1 cup dried papaya pieces
1 cup dried banana slices
1 cup dried kiwi fruit
2 cups dried strawberries
1 cup dried coconut flakes (or 3/4 cup grated coconut)
1/2 tbsp crystallized ginger (or 1/2 tbsp fresh, grated)
2 to 4 cups orange juice
1/2 cup orange liqueur (optional)
1/4 cup lemon juice (or about 1 lemon, juiced)

Combine and toss together the first seven ingredients.

Dry Fruit Medley

After combining the fruit, add 1/2 tbsp crystallized ginger. Serve dry mixture sprinkled over pineapple sherbet or coconut cream pie, or eat as a snack.

Moist Fruit Compote

After combining the fruit, add 2 tbsp fresh ginger, grated. Combine together about 2 cups of orange juice, the juice of one squeezed lemon, and the orange liqueur (if desired). Pour this juice mixture over the dried fruits and toss gently. Serve as a moist fruit cocktail, or as an appetizer or dessert.

SWEET DESSERT SOUP

1-1/2 cups dried apricots
3 cups raisins
1 cup dried apples
1-1/2 cups dried prunes
1 cup sugar
1/8 tsp salt
1/2 cup minute tapioca
2 tsp vanilla
4 tsp butter
2 tsp cinnamon

Cover fruit with salted water and boil until soft. Add remaining ingredients and enough water to make 1-1/2 quarts of liquid. Serve hot or cold.

FRUIT HORNS

3 eggs, beaten
1 cup plus 2 tbsp sugar
1 cup flour
1 tsp baking powder
Cream cheese and dried fruit filling (see **Candied Cream Cheese Teacakes**, page 116)

Combine first four ingredients with 2 tsp cold water. Drop tablespoonfuls onto a greased cookie sheet. Batter will spread. Bake at 350°F until light brown, approximately 12 minutes. Remove from oven and fold edges together while hot to form horn. Place seam side down to hold shape. Cool and fill with cream cheese filling. Makes 18 to 24 servings.

PERSIMMONY PUDDING

1 cup dried persimmons
1-1/4 cups flour
1 cup sugar
1-1/2 tsp soda
1/2 tsp salt
1-1/2 tsp baking powder
1-1/2 tsp butter or margarine
1/2 cup milk
1/2 cup oatmeal
1 cup chopped figs, raisins, or dates
1 cup chopped walnuts
1 tsp vanilla

Cover persimmons with 1/2 cup water, and allow to stand 20 minutes to rehydrate. Blend until pureed. Sift flour with sugar, soda, salt, and baking powder and combine with persimmons. Add the remaining ingredients, mixing thoroughly with each addition. Spoon batter into a 1-1/2 quart pudding mold; cover mold. Steam in covered kettle with boiling water half-way up the side of the mold for 3 hours. Serve hot.

RAISIN CUSTARD

3/4 cup sugar
2 tbsp cornstarch
1/4 tsp salt
2 cups milk
3 eggs, well beaten
2 tbsp butter
1 tsp vanilla
1/2 cup raisins (or dried cherries, blueberries, raspberries, or strawberries)

In a saucepan, blend together the sugar, cornstarch, salt, and your choice of fruit. Gradually stir in the milk, mixing well. Cook over medium heat until the mixture is smooth, thickened, and clear. Remove from the heat and quickly stir a small amount of hot pudding into the beaten eggs. Return the egg mixture to the hot pudding, mixing well. Return to heat (medium) and stir constantly to keep the pudding from sticking until it is thickened. Remove from the heat and add butter and vanilla. Stir until the butter is melted. Pour into serving dishes, and garnish with coconut or chopped nuts. Top with a dried fruit slice or a maraschino cherry. Chill. Makes 4 servings.

HIKING AND TRAIL MIX RECIPES

Note: All of the recipes within this section have been used extensively in the field, but almost any recipe, not requiring refrigeration, from our book or developed through your own experience may be perfectly suitable for the trail.

Granola and Snacks

P'NUTTY GRANOLA

4 cups rolled oats
1 cup chopped almonds, cashews, or peanuts
1/2 cup creamy peanut butter
1/2 cup honey
1/2 cup dried, powdered milk
1/2 cup raisins
1 cup other mixed dried fruit (pineapples, apples, figs, bananas, dates, etc.)
1/2 cup sesame seeds
1/2 cup sunflower seeds
1 cup large-flake dried coconut
1 tsp vanilla
1/2 tsp ground cinnamon

In a saucepan, thoroughly heat peanut butter and honey. Remove from heat and stir in cinnamon and vanilla. Combine oats, almonds, dry milk, sesame seeds, and sunflower seeds and place this dry mixture in a large, shallow roasting pan or on cookie sheets. Pour the warm peanut butter mixture over these dry ingredients and stir until coated. Spread mixture evenly about the pan. Bake at 300°F for about 30 minutes, or until lightly browned, stirring occasionally. Add the dried fruits and coconut after baking is complete. To dry, spread the mixture on trays and dehydrate overnight. When cooled, store granola in airtight containers. Makes about 10 cups. To make a "trail mix" or "gorp," simply add in carob chips or chocolate chips and additional dried fruits, nuts, seeds, etc.

NONNIE'S GREAT GRANOLA

4 cups rolled oats
1/2 cup wheat germ
1 cup brown sugar or 1/2 cup honey
2 cups coconut
1 cup sesame seeds
1 cup almonds and walnuts, chopped
1/2 cup wheat or soy flour
1 tsp vanilla
1 tsp cinnamon
1 cup oil
1 tsp salt

After dehydrating the above ingredients add:

1 cup raisins
1/2 cup dates
1/2 cup dried pineapple
1/2 cup dried apples
(or any combination of dried fruits)

Mix the first group of ingredients together in a large bowl and spread onto Teflex, kitchen parchment paper, or plastic wrap. Dehydrate at 145°F (approximately 3 hours) until crunchy. Add the second group of ingredients. Serve with milk or plain yogurt.

ZUCCHINI CHIPS

Cut zucchini into thin slices. Place on dehydrator trays and baste with barbecue sauce. Dehydrate until crisp. Additional snack chips can be made by sprinkling chips before they dry with seasoned salt, garlic salt, Parmesan cheese, or salad seasoning spices.

(Front) Fruit Leathers, pp. 125-126; (center) Strawberry Pancake Mix, p. 124, Raisin Biscuits, p. 125, Campfire Baking Mix, p. 124, P'Nutty Granola, p. 123, Smoked Honey Nuts, p. 124; and (rear) Vegetable Fish Chowder, p. 94.

TRAIL MIX

6 cups plain granola
2 cups sunflower seeds
1 cup carob or chocolate chips
1/4 cup raisins
1/2 cup diced apricots
1/2 cup diced pears
1/2 cup broken cashews
1/2 cup coconut strips (pared)
1/2 cup diced apples
1/2 cup diced peaches
1/2 cup slivered almonds
1 cup dried tomato chips

Combine the above ingredients. This is a nutritional TV snack and makes a lovely gift package when placed in a compote. It is also great for hiking.

SMOKED HONEY NUTS

4 cups nuts
1 tbsp honey
1/4 tsp liquid smoke
1 tbsp salt
3/4 cup water

Marinate nuts for 45 minutes in honey, smoke, salt, and water mixture. Drain well. Place on Teflex, kitchen parchment paper, or plastic wrap covered trays and dry for 3 hours at 145°F.

Baking and Soup Mixes

DRIED FRUIT SNACK

1/2 cup raisins
1/2 cup dried apricots
1/2 cup dried pears
1 cup dried bananas
1 cup dried coconut flakes
1/2 cup dried dates
1/2 cup dried strawberries

Chop the ingredients and mix together. Store in an airtight container.

STRAWBERRY PANCAKES

3/4 cup shortening
3 cups campfire baking mix (recipe given below)
1 tbsp powdered egg
1 tbsp sugar
1/2 cup dried strawberries
1 cup water

Combine all ingredients, cutting in shortening. Stir until ingredients are moistened. If batter is thick, add a little more water to thin. Drop by spoonfuls on a hot, greased griddle. Turn when bubbles appear on top. Serve piping hot with butter and syrup or try sprinkling with powdered sugar.

CINNAMON PECANS

4 cups pecans
2 tbsp honey
1/2 tsp cinnamon
1 tbsp salt
1/2 tsp nutmeg
3/4 cup water

Marinate nuts in honey, water, and spice mixture for 45 minutes. Arrange in a single layer on dehydrator trays covered with Teflex, kitchen parchment paper, or plastic wrap. Dry for 5 hours at 145°F.

CAMPFIRE BAKING MIX

3 cups whole wheat flour
3 cups unbleached white flour
1 cup wheat germ
4 cups old-fashioned rolled oats
2 cups dried, powdered milk
4 tbsp baking powder
1 tbsp salt

Combine dry ingredients. Divide into eight plastic freezer bags and seal. Add 1/4 cup shortening to each cup dry mix just before using. Makes 13 cups.

RAISIN BISCUITS

1/2 cup shortening
2 cups campfire baking mix (recipe given on previous
    page)
1/2 cup raisins (or dried blueberries)
water

Cut shortening into baking mix. Add raisins and enough water to make a stiff dough. Divide into 8 pieces, roll each into a ball with your hands; then flatten slightly. Place on a piece of ungreased aluminum foil and bake over hot coals approximately 15 to 30 minutes, depending on the temperature of your fire.

TOMATO-RICE SOUP MIX

1/2 cup rice
2 tbsp dried onions
1 cup powdered tomatoes
1/4 cup tomato pieces
1 red chili pepper

Add ingredients to 4 cups water and boil until rice is tender. Remove chili pepper and serve. Serves 4.

INSTANT SOUP MIXES

Puree any thick home-made or canned soup, such as lentil, navy bean, split pea, etc., until smooth. Spread pureed soup onto Teflex, kitchen parchment paper, or plastic wrap and dry into a leather. As an alternate drying method, drop spoonfuls of the mixture onto the Teflex, kitchen parchment paper, or plastic wrap and dry into chips or wafers. To prepare a hot "instant" soup, tear off the desired amount of leather and place it or the desired number of soup chips into a bowl or cup. Add boiling water, stir, and allow to steep for a few minutes until soup returns to its original consistency.

INSTANT SOUP CUP

1 tsp dried, powdered vegetables (such as peas)
4 tsp dried milk
1 cup boiling water

Grind dried vegetables into a powder using a blender set at the highest speed. Mix powder with dried milk. Place in cup and add boiling water. Stir, and season to taste. For better flavor, soup may be simmered.

Fruit Leathers

BANANA BLUSH LEATHER

1 cup strawberries
1 banana

Puree fruit in blender. Pour onto Teflex, kitchen parchment paper, or plastic wrap, and dehydrate at 135°F until leathery.

PEACHY PEAR LEATHER

1 cup peaches, peeled
1/2 cup pears, peeled

Blend together and sweeten if desired. Pour on Teflex, kitchen parchment paper, or plastic wrap and dehydrate at 135°F until leathery.

PERSIMMON-PINEAPPLE LEATHER

1 cup persimmon pulp
1/2 cup crushed or fresh pineapple pieces

Puree in blender. Spread on Teflex, kitchen parchment paper, or plastic wrap and dehydrate at 135°F until leathery.

BANANA-PEANUT BUTTER LEATHER

4 cups ripe bananas (pureed)
1 cup old-fashioned peanut butter
1 tsp vanilla

Blend banana puree, peanut butter, and vanilla together. Spread mixture onto Teflex, kitchen parchment paper, or plastic wrap and dry until leathery. To create peanut butter candy bits, pour melted chocolate or carob chips over the dried leather, roll up, and cut into 1" pieces. Serve as a natural candy.

APRICOT-CHERRY LEATHER

1 cup apricots
1/2 cup cherries
honey or sugar to taste

Puree apricots with a small amount of water. Add cherries and sweetener; blend and pour onto Teflex, kitchen parchment paper, or plastic wrap. Dehydrate at 135°F until leathery.

CRANAPPLE LEATHER

1 cup apples, chopped
1/2 cup cranberries
honey or sugar to taste

Puree apples in blender with a small amount of water. Add cranberries and sweetener if desired. Pour on Teflex, kitchen parchment paper, or plastic wrap covered dehydrator trays and dry at 135°F until leathery.

CHEWY FRUIT ROLLS

Use any fruit leather recipe. Dehydrate at 135°F until tacky. Remove from Teflex, kitchen parchment paper, or plastic wrap and sprinkle with coconut or top with melted carob, thinly spread peanut butter, or cream cheese. Roll tightly and cut into finger-sized lengths. Keep refrigerated. Fruit rolls are great as a snack or lunch box treat.

Meats, Marinades, and Mixes

BEEF AND POULTRY JERKY MARINADES

The following marinades are especially good for beef and poultry jerky recipes. These marinades can be used for 3 to 4 pounds of beef or poultry.

Teriyaki Marinade

1 cup soy sauce
2 crushed garlic cloves
2 tsp crushed or ground ginger root
2 tbsp brown sugar
1 tsp pepper

Combine and mix the above ingredients.

Barbecue Sauce Marinade

1 tbsp oil
1/4 cup dried onion flakes
1/4 tsp dried garlic, powdered
1/2 tsp salt
1/2 tsp chili powder
1/2 tsp dry mustard
2-1/2 tbsp brown sugar
2 tbsp Worcestershire sauce
8 oz can tomato sauce, or 2 tbsp tomato powder plus
    1 cup water
1/2 cup dry red wine, or 1/4 cup red wine vinegar plus
    1/4 cup lemon juice

Sauté onion flakes in vegetable oil. Stir in garlic, salt, chili powder, dry mustard, and brown sugar; add the Worcestershire sauce, tomato sauce, and wine and stir well. Bring mixture to boil and then simmer for 5 minutes. Cool. Makes 2 cups of marinade.

SWEET AND SOUR MARINADE

1 cup pineapple juice
1/2 cup lemon juice
1/2 cup red wine
2 tbsp soy sauce
1 tbsp onion flakes
1 tbsp brown sugar
1/2 tsp garlic
1/2 tsp peppers
1/2 tsp oregano

Combine and mix the above ingredients.

CIDERED VENISON JERKY MARINADE

1 to 2 lbs raw, lean venison strips
1/4 cup cider vinegar
4 tbsp Worcestershire sauce
2 tbsp brown sugar
1 tsp salt
1 tsp dried garlic powder
1/2 tsp pepper

Place all ingredients in a flat dish or bowl. Cover and refrigerate 8 hours or overnight, turning strips often. Drain and place strips on dehydrator trays. Dry until hard.

MRS. ANDREW'S ENGLISH MARINADE

1 cup dry red wine
2/3 cup light salad oil
1 clove minced garlic
1 small lemon, thinly sliced
2 tsp dried parsley flakes
1 tsp oregano
1/2 tsp salt
1/4 tsp crushed fennel seeds
1/4 tsp pepper

Combine and mix the above ingredients. This marinade can be used with fish or beef.

BASIC JERKY RECIPE

3 to 4 lbs lean beef (cut into strips)
1/2 cup tomato sauce base or catsup
1/4 cup soy sauce
1/4 cup Worcestershire sauce
1 tsp onion powder or 2 tsp onion flakes
1 tsp garlic powder
1/2 tsp cracked pepper
1/2 tsp hickory smoke flavoring or salt

Blend all ingredients and soak meat strips in mixture. Keep refrigerated 6 to 12 hours, stirring and turning meat occasionally in marinade. Once meat is marinated to desired strength, drain off marinade and dry.

POTLESS STEW

2 cups dried beef, turkey, or chicken cubes
2 cups sliced dried potatoes
1-1/2 cups dried green beans
1 cup sliced dried onion rings
1 cup dried carrot slices
2 cups dried tomato slices
1 cup dried mushrooms
3/4 cup dried, chopped celery
4 beef bouillon cubes
4 cups water
4 tbsp flour

Mix all but the last three ingredients and divide onto four pieces of heavy-duty aluminum foil and seal, leaving a small opening. Combine bouillon cubes, water, and flour; pour equally into each of the four packages. Cook over coals for 1 to 2 hours. Serve in foil packages. (Packages may also be heated in the oven or on a barbeque grill.)

HANGTOWN MIX

1 cup dry red wine
2/3 cup oil
2 tbsp onion flakes
2 tbsp Worcestershire sauce
2 tsp tomato powder
1 tsp cayenne
1/2 tsp cumin

Combine the above ingredients and thoroughly mix.

SPICY DRIED FISH CURE

1 lb salt
1/2 lb dark brown sugar
1 tbsp saltpeter
1 tbsp white pepper
2 tsp garlic powder
2 tsp onion powder
Plus optional crushed spices:
    bay leaf, cloves, allspice, and mace

Mix ingredients and let stand for 24 hours. Then wash fish and soak in salt brine to remove blood. Pat fish dry and sprinkle on dry cure, then dehydrate. One pound of dry cure will coat 10 to 12 pounds of fish.

DRINKS, BREADS, AND MORE

Drinks

CRANBERRY TEA

1 cup dried cranberries
5 quarts water
2-1/2 cups sugar
3/4 cup cinnamon red hots
2 whole cloves
2 cups orange juice
juice from three lemons

Cook cranberries in 1 quart water to extract the juice. Strain cranberries, reserving juice only. Cook 1 quart water, sugar, red hots, and cloves until dissolved to liquid. Add cranberry juice, orange juice, lemon juice, and 3 quarts hot water. Strain through cheesecloth to obtain clear liquid. Makes 1 gallon.

MARDI GRAS PUNCH

1/4 cup dried lemon rind (about 3 lemons)
1/4 cup dried orange rind (about 3 oranges)
1/4 cup allspice berries
1/4 cup whole cloves
10 to 12 (3") cinnamon sticks (broken up)
1 tsp nutmeg

Mix together all ingredients and place in an airtight container until ready to use. Store in a cool, dark place. To prepare punch, add 1 teaspoon punch mix to each cup of apple cider. Heat to boiling, simmer 5 to 10 minutes, strain, and serve. Fruit punches, lemonade, orange juice, and tea can be used in place of cider.

RHUBARB PUNCH

3 cups dried rhubarb
3 cups water
12 oz can frozen lemonade
12 oz can frozen orange juice
1 cup sugar or 3/4 cup honey
1 quart ginger ale

Rehydrate rhubarb by placing in a pan with water and simmering 5 minutes. Cool, puree in blender, and add remaining ingredients.

BAHAMA SLUSH

4 cups sugar
6 cups water
1 small can orange juice, concentrated
3 small cans water
2 tbsp lemon juice
lemon-lime soda
2-1/2 cups banana chips (softened in 1-1/2 cups water)

Boil sugar and 6 cups water for 3 minutes and cool. Add fruit juices, additional water, and bananas. Freeze mixture. To use, blend equal parts of slush with soda.

129

(Left to right): Yogurt, p. 110; and Spicy Potpourri, p. 134.

APRICOT LIQUEUR

dried apricots to fill 1 quart jar three-quarters full,
    unpacked
1 cup sugar
1 pint vodka or brandy

Add sugar and vodka to apricots in jar. Cover and let stand at room temperature from 2 weeks to 8 months. Turn jar upside down every other day. Strain liquid through three thicknesses of cheesecloth for clarity. Other dried fruits such as peaches or cherries can be used.

CAMOMILE-MINT TEA

3 tbsp dried mint leaves
1 tbsp dried camomile
1 quart water

Add peppermint and camomile to boiling water and brew for 10 minutes. Strain and serve sweetened or with lemon. Makes 1 quart.

ROSE HIP TEA

1/2 cup dried rose hips
1/4 cup dried lemon thyme
1 quart water

Simmer rose hips in water for 1 hour. Strain through two layers of cheesecloth to clarify. Steep lemon thyme; then strain and add to rose hips. Makes 1 quart.

CRANBERRY-APPLE DRINK

1/2 cup dried apples
1/4 cup dried cranberries
sweetener (to taste)
water

Add all ingredients to blender with 1/2 cup water and mix. Serve cold over ice or hot with a cinnamon stick and orange slices. Makes 1 serving.

Breads and Snacks

CORN BREAD

1 cup finely ground cornmeal
1 cup flour
1/4 cup sugar
4 tsp baking powder
1/2 tsp salt
1 egg
1 cup milk
1/4 cup soft shortening

Combine all ingredients. Pour into an 8″ square pan or a 6-muffin tin. Bake at 425°F for 20 to 25 minutes.

PINEAPPLE-PECAN BREAKFAST BREAD

1 cup chopped pecans
3/4 cup chopped dates (pitted)
1-1/2 tsp dried orange peel, minced (rehydrated in 2 tsp water)
2-1/3 cups flour
1 tsp baking powder
1 tsp baking soda
1/4 tsp salt
3/4 cup sugar
1/4 cup margarine or butter, softened
1 egg
1/2 cup dried pineapple pieces (rehydrated in 1-1/2 cups water)

Combine 1 tablespoon flour, pecans, dates, and rehydrated orange peel; toss well and set aside. Combine remaining flour, baking powder, baking soda, and salt (in small bowl); set aside. Cream sugar and butter until smooth and fluffy; add egg and beat until blended. Add flour mixture gradually to the creamed butter mixture, alternating with the rehydrated pineapple mixture. Stir in floured fruit and nuts and pour into well-greased large loaf pan (9″ × 5″ × 3″). Bake for about 1 hour at 350°F or until bread tests done. Cool slightly if desired. Makes 1 loaf.

CARROT DATE BREAD

1/2 cup corn oil
3/4 cup sugar
1-3/4 cups flour
2-1/2 tsp baking powder
1/2 tsp salt
1 tsp cinnamon
1 cup shredded dehydrated carrots
2 eggs
1/2 cup chopped dates

In blender bowl, place 1 cup shredded carrots and cover with water. Let stand for 10 minutes and then puree to smooth consistency. Add corn oil and sugar. Add eggs, one at a time, blending after each addition. Mix in all remaining ingredients except dates. Blend. Stir in dates. Pour into a greased 8-1/2″ x 4-1/2″ x 2-1/2″ loaf pan. Bake at 350°F for 55 to 60 minutes.

NUTTY BANANA BREAD

1-1/8 cups dried banana slices
2 cups unsifted flour
1-2/3 cups sugar
1-1/4 tsp baking powder
1-1/4 tsp baking soda
1 tsp salt
2/3 cup shortening
2/3 cup buttermilk
2 eggs
1/2 cup crunchy peanut butter

Reconstitute dehydrated banana slices in an equal amount of water; let soak for 1 hour. Thoroughly stir together the flour, sugar, baking powder, baking soda, and salt. Add shortening and beat 2 minutes. Add eggs and beat an additional 2 minutes. Mix in bananas with half of buttermilk and beat 2 minutes more. Add rest of liquid and peanut butter; blend until smooth. Pour into greased 9″ x 5″ x 3″ loaf pan. Bake in pre-heated 350°F oven until toothpick comes out clean, approximately 50 to 70 minutes. Let stand on wire rack for 10 minutes, loosen edges, and turn out on rack; turn right side up to cool.

PUMPKIN DESSERT BREAD

3-1/2 cups flour
2 tsp soda
1-1/2 tsp salt
1 tsp cinnamon
1/2 tsp cloves
1 tsp nutmeg
3 cups sugar
4 beaten eggs
1 cup oil
1 cup dried pumpkin
2/3 cup cold water

Reconstitute pumpkin in warm water. Mix all ingredients together and beat well. Pour into five greased dessert loaf pans. Bake at 350°F for 40 minutes until done.

WHEAT BREAD

1 package dry yeast
2 cups warm water
2 tbsp sugar
2 tsp salt
4 cups white flour
1/2 cup hot water
1/2 cup brown sugar, packed
3 tbsp shortening
4 cups whole wheat flour

Place yeast in warm water. Add sugar, salt, and white flour. Beat until smooth. Cover and put in warm dehydrator until light in color and bubbles appear on top of dough, approximately 1 hour.

Combine hot water, brown sugar, and shortening. Cool to lukewarm. Add to yeast mixture. Now add whole wheat flour and mix until smooth. Turn dough out onto lightly floured surface. Knead about 10 minutes using a little wheat flour on your hands until dough loses its stickiness. Place dough into greased bowl; turn over once to grease top of dough. Cover. Let rise in warm dehydrator until double.

Punch down dough. Cut in half with knife. Shape each half to form a ball; cover and let rise 10 minutes. Place into lightly-greased loaf pans, cover, and let rise until double. Bake at 375°F approximately 40 to 50 minutes.

CRANBERRY-APPLE BREAD

1-1/2 cups butter
1 cup sugar
2 eggs
1 tsp vanilla
2 cups flour
1/2 tsp salt
1 tsp baking soda
1/3 cup orange juice
1/2 cup dried apples
1/4 cup dried cranberries

Reconstitute apples and cranberries in warm water. Cream butter and sugar. Add eggs and vanilla and beat well. Add dry ingredients alternately with orange juice. Fold in apples and cranberries and pour into greased loaf pan. Bake at 350°F for 55 minutes.

BANANA-FIG BREAD

1 cup chopped dried figs (about 15 dried figs)
1 cup sugar
1/2 cup (one stick) butter or margarine
2 eggs
1 cup dried banana slices (rehydrated)
1 tbsp lemon juice
2 cups whole wheat flour
3 tsp baking powder
1/2 tsp salt

Thoroughly combine sugar and butter. Add eggs, one at a time, beating well after each addition. Puree banana slices, and stir into the sugar and butter mixture along with the lemon juice. Combine the flour, baking powder, and salt, and add this to the mixture. Stir in figs. Place mixture in a 9″ × 5″ × 3″ bread pan at 350°F for 1 hour or until bread is brown and toothpick inserted into bread comes out dry. Cool on rack and serve. Mixture makes 1 loaf.

HERB BUTTER

1/2 cup butter
1/2 cup oil
1 tbsp dried parsley flakes
1/2 tsp dried thyme
1-1/2 tsp dried basil
1/4 tsp dried chives
1/4 tsp salt
1/8 tsp pepper
1/8 tsp garlic powder

Mix all the ingredients in blender; blend until smooth and creamy. Spread on crackers or warm fresh bread. Makes 1 cup.

FRUIT BUTTER

2 lbs dried fruit (apricots, peaches, pears, or apples)
6 cups water
2 cups sugar
1 tsp cinnamon
1 tsp almond extract

Place dried fruit and water in a large pan and bring to a boil. Cover and simmer 30 minutes. Stir in sugar, cinnamon, and almond extract. Cover and simmer 30 minutes longer, stirring occasionally. When fruit has become soft, remove the mixture from the heat and allow to cool. Pour fruit and juices in a blender and puree. Store in covered jars in the refrigerator. Use "butter" as a filling for cookies and muffins or spread on toast. Makes 1 quart.

POPOVERS WITH PIZZAZZ

1 cup milk
3 eggs
2 tsp butter
1/2 tsp salt
1 cup flour, sifted
1 tsp mixed herbs—parsley, chives, and powdered onions
1/4 cup Parmesan cheese

Add cheese and spices to flour. Combine ingredients in a bowl in the order listed and blend until smooth. Pour into greased popover pan, filling halfway. Bake at 400°F for 35 minutes, until crisp and brown.

SPICY PINEAPPLE-PUMPKIN MUFFINS

1-1/2 cups flour, unsifted (may use part whole wheat)
1/2 cup sugar (or 1/4 cup honey)
2 tsp baking powder
3/4 tsp salt
1 tsp ground cinnamon
1/2 tsp ground ginger
1/4 tsp ground cloves
1/2 cup dried pineapple bits
1 egg
1 cup milk or cream
1/2 cup dried, chopped pumpkin (reconstituted)
1/4 cup vegetable oil
3 tsp sugar
3/4 tsp cinnamon

Pour milk over pumpkin and let reconstitute; set aside. In large bowl mix together the flour, sugar, baking powder, salt, and spices. Mix in the dried pineapple bits and coat with flour mixture. In small bowl add reconstituted pumpkin and beat with egg and oil until smooth and creamy. Stir this egg mixture into the flour mixture, mixing just until combined. Fill muffin pans two-thirds full; sprinkle with cinnamon-sugar mixture. Bake for about 20 to 25 minutes until browned. Makes 12 muffins.

HONEY SQUARES

2 eggs
3/4 cup honey
1/2 cup whole wheat flour
1/4 tsp salt
1/2 cup ground granola
1 cup raisins or ground cherries, dates, or prunes
1 cup chopped dried nuts

Beat eggs until light and fluffy. Gradually add honey; heat if necessary to pour in a thin stream. Add flour, granola, and salt. Stir in dried fruits and nuts, and pour into a greased 8″ square baking pan. Bake at 325°F for approximately 45 minutes or until brown and firm in center. Cut in squares while still warm. Cool. Makes 16 squares.

Beauty Aids and Potpourri

MINT TEA BATH

4 tbsp loose (non herbal) dried tea (or 5 or so tea bags, opened)
5 cups boiling water
4 tbsp dried mint leaves (any variety of mint works well)

Steep dried tea in 4 cups of boiling water for about 15 minutes. Steep the dried mint leaves in 1 cup of boiling water for a few minutes. Mix tea and mint leaves together and pour into a warm bath.

STRAWBERRY COMPLEXION CREAM

1/2 cup dried strawberries
1/2 cup water
1/4 cup wheat germ oil
2 tbsp rolled oats (dry oatmeal)

Rehydrate strawberries in water for 3 minutes; mash well. Meanwhile, finely crush oatmeal in a blender (to resemble flour). In saucepan, stir in the mashed strawberries, oil, and oatmeal. Simmer over low heat, stirring constantly, until mixture is thickened. Place in covered, airtight container (glass, ceramic, or plastic) and refrigerate until ready to use.

GERRY'S LAVENDER POTPOURRI

1 cup lavender blossoms
2 cups lemon verbena leaves
2 tsp orrisroot powder
1 cup pink rose petals
1 cup white carnation petals

Dry petals in dehydrator at 95°F until crisp. Lightly mix flowers in a bowl and sprinkle with orrisroot powder (a preservative). Store in jars for 1 month in a cool, dark place. Then place in decorator jars.

JASMINE POTPOURRI

2 cups jasmine flowers
1 cup scented geranium leaves
1 cup citrus blossoms
8 drops oil of vanilla
1 tsp benzoin or 1 tsp orrisroot powder

Dry, mix, and store as with **Lavender Potpourri**.

MINT POTPOURRI

1 cup mint leaves
1 cup lavender flowers
1-1/2 tsp cloves
1-1/2 tsp nutmeg
1-1/3 tsp coriander
1 tsp orrisroot powder

Dry, mix, and store as with **Lavender Potpourri**.

SPRINGTIME POTPOURRI

3 cups dried rose petals (red, pink, yellow)
1 cup dried lavender flowers
1 cup dried calendulas
1 cup dried pansy heads
1 cup dried bachelor buttons or cornflowers
2 tbsp combined spices—cloves, nutmeg, and allspice
1 tbsp orrisroot powder
10 drops rose oil (optional)

Dry, mix, and store as for **Lavender Potpourri**.

SPICY POTPOURRI

1 quart dried roses, mixed colors
3/4 cup dried lavender flowers
1 tsp powdered cinnamon
1 tsp nutmeg
1 tsp allspice
1 tsp cloves
1 tbsp dried rosemary
1 tbsp benzoin (preservative) or 1 tbsp orrisroot powder
10 drops oil of jasmine

Lightly mix all ingredients as with **Lavender Potpourri**, add oil of jasmine for a long-lasting fragrance, and store.

INDEX